MORRISSEY'S MANCHESTER

THE ESSENTIAL SMITHS TOUR

PHILL GATENBY

SECOND EDITION

EMPIRE
PUBLICATIONS

EMPIRE PUBLICATIONS
1 Newton Street, Manchester M1 1HW
© Phill Gatenby 2002, 2009

ISBN 1 901 746 56 9

Cover design and layout: Ashley Shaw

Printed in Great Britain by
CPI Cox & Wyman, Reading, RG1 8EX.

TO DAD

CHARLES GEOFFREY GATENBY, 1931 - 2007

*"The hour or the day no one can tell,
but one day 'goodbye' will be 'farewell'"*

CONTENTS

ABOUT THE AUTHOR

Phill Gatenby was born in Lancashire in 1963. Educated at Manchester Polytechnic, he also graduated from the world of football fanzines, contributing to 'Blue Print' (1988-92) then producing his own 'This Charming Fan' between 1992 - 96.

Having contributed to several football compilation books in the 1990s, 'Morrissey's Manchester' became Phill's first book (2002) and followed this up in 2007 with 'Panic On The Streets' - The Smiths & Morrissey UK Location Guide' (Reynolds & Hearn Ltd). In 2008, he was the ghost writer for 'Sully' (Empire Publications).

He works alongside Inspiral Carpets drummer, Craig Gill, with 'Manchester Music Tours'. Phill and Craig are currently writing the definitive 'Manchester music guide', which should be out soon.

Phill is also writing a complete guide to the

'Madchester' scene that may also be published soon, with about three or four other books in his head that keep him awake at night!

He lives in north Manchester and has two daughters, Rohannah and Leah and one grand daughter, Phoebe.

He saw The Smiths five times and his latest Morrissey count is thirty-six!

To contact Phill / Craig

www.manchestermusictours.com

www.myspace.com/mancmusictour

ACKNOWLEDGEMENTS
TO CERTAIN PEOPLE I KNOW:

THANKS TO ALL at Empire for believing in the book - John, Ash, Stuart and Mike as well as Paul in the shop. I'm still waiting for the 'Gold Disc' for 10,000 sales!

Continued thanks to Peter Finan, Simon Goddard and Grim O' Grady for always being at the end of an email each time I ask a further question.

Craig Gill - one day we will be running three double decker buses a day around Manchester!

David Tseng, for his wonderful website 'Morrissey-Solo.com' for enabling me to promote the books, tours and calendars too!

Leslie Holmes and all at Salford Lads Club for welcoming fans from around the world.

To all friends at the Star & Garter: Andy the boss and Dave the DJ. Kathy, Clare, Mel & Brendan, Paul & Andy, Adam, Nigel, Ami, Ann & Gemma, Deano, Stevie & Sara, Natalie, Kirsty & Keith, Nick the Villa fan, Ben Budd, Mike, Darren the Geordie from Leeds, The 'Derby Four', Michelle, Clare and Annaliese

Fans further afield: Fergus and family in Dublin,

Debs in California for maintaining the myspace page, Andrea & Chris in Pennsylvania, Big Keith in Maryland, Art, Efren and Elvira in Los Angeles, Veronica in Argentina, Diane in New York, Natalie & Tommi and Simone in Germany. Oh yeah, and a BIG shout for Alida, Kath and Steven in Massachusettes. Thanks also to Mark Taylor for the foreword.

To friends Jim & Linda Ferris, Loz Murphy & Kim, Collette Walsh and Gilly (my official stalker), George, Harpal, Ray, and 'the beast', for all round general support and more importantly friendship.

To Peter (again), Tess, Hayley, Kraig and Kewpie - collectively known as 'The Suedeheads'.

To The Gatenby's - Mum, Rohannah, Leah, Phoebe, Malcolm, Sheena, Ian and Grace.

FOREWORD

PUNCTURED BICYCLE BY MARK TAYLOR

WHEN YOU ARE the 18-year-old editor of a Smiths fanzine, the last thing you expect is a call from the band's press officer asking for help with the next video shoot.

It was September 1987 when I got the out-of-the-blue call from Pat Bellis - Rough Trade press officer, Smiths photographer and Morrissey confidante. Pat and I had corresponded several times over the previous year or so and she was the conduit between the band and my fanzine, *Smiths Indeed*.

Until that point, Pat had been the person who could get me photos of the band (hard copy prints which were sent by post for me to have scanned in - this was long before email and the internet) and the person who would get my letters through to Morrissey and vice versa.

But then she got in touch to say that Morrissey wanted to find 12 Smiths fans to join him in Manchester to film the video for the forthcoming single 'I Started Something I Couldn't Finish'.

The video was to be a tour of Morrissey's

Manchester - landmarks from Smiths photos and lyrics - with Mozzer cycling around them with his dozen lookalikes.

At this point, *Smiths Indeed* was the biggest selling Smiths fanzine around. It was essentially the 'official' fanzine for the band, being sold on the band's merchandise stall at gigs.

I had built up a formidable address book of Smiths fans and it wasn't difficult to pick a dozen of the most dedicated Morrissey followers and ask them if they wanted to be in the next video. As if I needed to wait for them to reply by return of post!

A month later, on Sunday October 18, the 12 fans made the journey to Manchester to meet Morrissey and the film crew. I was invited to join them but decided to stand in the shadows and report on it for the fanzine and take photographs.

It was, naturally, a wet and bitterly cold day in Manchester and we congregated at a city centre hotel at 9am. The 12 fans had all brought their own bikes, apart from two who had travelled a considerable distance by train. All had Smiths t-shirts, quiffs and NHS specs. It was quite a sight.

The first location was a semi-derelict block of flats in Hulme, where the fans had to cycle down a spiralling footpath. There was still no sign of Morrissey.

At midday, the crew moved back to the hotel where Morrissey emerged to greet the rather nervous people involved.

Over the next six hours, Morrissey and the 'extras' moved around the city to film several scenes: outside

Victoria Station, a bridge with a sign pointing to Strangeways/Deansgate/Salford and Cheetham Hill, Strangeways Prison, Coronation Street, Stephen Street, Salford Lads' Club, the old Albert Finney betting shop in Salford.

As a bystander, it made for fascinating viewing and Morrissey frequently came over for chats between takes. I remember one of them being about how he had found the cover artwork for The Queen Is Dead and he seeming quite impressed when I told him I also had the very magazine in which he had spotted the original picture.

Just after 6pm, we all returned to the hotel and Morrissey signed autographs for several minutes, chatting to the lookalikes and having pictures taken with them.

The small black and white picture of me with Morrissey on that extraordinary day remains one of my most treasured possessions 22 years later. It was an unforgettable experience, especially as The Smiths were no more only weeks after that rainy day in Manchester.

Even more memorable was the fact that I was offered a lift back to Bristol with Morrissey in his chauffer-driven car (he was recording near Bath at the time) but had to decline because I suffered from terrible travel sickness at the time and was too afraid of embarrassing myself en route.

It still ranks as one of the biggest, most stupid mistakes of my life.

The full account of the filming of I Started Something I Couldn't Finish appears in issue six of

Smiths Indeed, which has been reprinted as part of the complete set of 12 issues of Smiths Indeed.

For more information, contact me at: <u>markfoodie@btinternet.com</u>

INTRODUCTION

WELCOME TO THE second (and updated) edition of "Morrissey's Manchester", your complete guide to ensuring that your visit to the home of Morrissey & The Smiths is a truly unforgettable experience.

Why the second edition? Well, for two reasons:

Firstly because the original run of 10,000 copies has almost sold out and the book is still popular and in demand.

Secondly, Manchester has changed quite a lot since 2002 when the book was first published. Some of the sites on the tours are no longer there and new places to visit have been added. Simply reprinting the original book would have been a wasted opportunity and also a disservice to those buying it and visiting Manchester.

So what is new? In 2002, Morrissey had only played one solo gig in his home town. Since then he has played locally on ten occasions, using four venues not featured in the first edition. There is also a new song reference, a couple of name changes to some of the sites and a couple of places I missed out first time around!

Sadly, one of my favourite sites in the book is no

longer there. I refer to the mosaic (above) that was on
the side of Afflecks Palace. The 25 year lease on the
building had expired in 2008 and was not renewed by
the owners. At one point it was feared the building
would be turned into offices or apartments. After
demonstrations by local people and meetings with
the city council, the building (and businesses) was
saved but the name was changed to 'Afflecks' and the

mosiacs on the outside of the building were taken down by the previous lease holders, put in storage and haven't re-appeared! When working in the city centre, I would pass the mosiacs on a daily basis, always giving them a glance as I passed by. They were iconic symbols of the city and are greatly missed.

The book has given me quite an adventure and many memorable times. The first edition was written on a week-long holiday in Crete during October 2001. I say holiday, but I never left my apartment except for the daily trip to the local supermarket for food and (more importantly) beers. In 2008, I appeared on the BBC2 quiz show 'Eggheads' alongside four other Smiths/Morrissey fans (called 'The Suedeheads'). On my final question, which I needed to answer correctly to take Judith to a sudden death round, I incorrectly gave the answer that Crete was further east than fellow Greek Isle Rhodes. Had I left my hotel room more often that week in 2002 and explored my surroundings, I may have got the question right!

I could also write a book on the five day visit to Los Angeles in 2003, when I accompanied the publisher's then Managing Editor, Stuart Fish, to the annual Morrissey convention. We bumped into Prince in Hollywood and I drove around LA / Hollywood on the final day in a Jeep belonging to a very drunk young woman (who I'd never met before or since), who, had I not taken the keys from her, would have happily driven herself...

Stuart: 'You can't drive her car'

Me: 'Well would you rather she drove?'

Stuart: 'That's a good point...'

I did finally allow her to drive her car.... but only because we had arrived at LAX to catch the flight back home and she got out from the very tight and cramped space mascarading as a back seat. We were a little late at the airport, and made a hasty exit from the car... so, Christine, thanks for the loan of the car and sorry the goodbye was a bit brief!

In between all this, Stuart's friend Brian had driven to meet us from Phoenix and Stuart gave him the instant job title of 'Empire Publication's Only USA Sales Representative'. Brian was so pleased with this job title that he agreed to take one suitcase containing 250 books back with him to Phoenix (so we didn't have to take it home!). If anyone out there knows a Brian in Phoenix, could you ask him if we can have our books (and suitcase) back please?

The book has also given me a few media appearances too. I appeared in the Granada TV documentary (2002) 'These Things Take Time' (celebrating the 20th anniversary of The Smiths first gig) and I was filmed outside The Ritz, the cemetery gates and on the iron bridge.

I even managed to get a brief (unplanned) appearance on the 'Who Put The M In Manchester' DVD (2004), in the extras section, outside The Salford Lads Club. I was involved with organising a charity bike ride to raise money for The Salford Lads Club in 2007, the 16 miles we rode taking in the route of The MozBus (of which more later) and an interview was given on the local Granada news programme and an appearance on the rival BBC news too.

Finally, in 2009, Manchester's Channel M featured

the Manchester Music Tours. The music tours has probably been the biggest enjoyment coming from the book. When Morrissey announced he was to play at the MEN Arena in 2004, I was getting emails asking me to 'put something on'. The result was 'The MozBus' - a coach full of fans from all corners of the earth, being driven through the streets of Manchester, Salford and Trafford, causing confusion and amusement at the same time, to local people as to why 50 people have got off a coach on Kings Road in Stretford, just to climb up an iron bridge, walk along it, take a photograph (maybe add a bit more graffiti) and get back on the bus! I did two trips that weekend - the Saturday afternoon prior to the gig and the previous evening too, dropping everyone off at the Star & Garter at the end.

At The Salford Lads Club, there was a treat waiting as Andy Rourke with Vinny Peculiar played five songs acoustically - three of which were Smiths songs! On the Friday evening, Linder Sterling was outside filming scenes that became the extras for the aforementioned DVD. On the Saturday, the NME came on board with a reporter and photographer and the MozBus was given a whole page in the following week's edition.

Since then, the MozBus rode again a few months later when Morrissey appeared at the Move Festival at Lancashire County Cricket ground and the following year after a weekend of Smiths & Morrissey related synopsis' at Manchester University.

The MozBus was resurrected for the Manchester Apollo gigs in May 2009, this time (and finally) fans were driven around on a double decker bus - the disco bus belonging to Sankey's nightclub - complete with a downstairs dancefloor.

In between the bus trips, small groups and individuals were getting in touch and requesting personal tours. I teamed up with Craig Gill, drummer with Madchester band 'The Inspiral Carpets', and we began tours of not just Smiths & Morrissey related places, but Manchester music in general, covering Joy Division / New Order and Oasis, among others. In the summer months there are walking tours of the city centre's music related venues, which has grown steadily and healthily.

For more details visit either link:

www.manchestermusictours.com

www.myspace.com/mancmusictour

Through films such as 'Twenty-Four Hour Party People' and 'Control', Manchester is finally waking up to the fact that there is a rich musical heritage in and around the city and the time is right to celebrate that. Although the city may never become a musical heritage theme park (like Liverpool or Memphis), there is enough demand and places to go to satisfy those visitors to the city seeking out the musical past and exploring it as they wish. I enjoy the personal tours as it is great to spend time with visitors to the city from all over the world and I get a buzz off the excitement they display when taking them to the places that influenced Morrissey & The Smiths - places that shaped the words and music to songs that mean so much to so many.

As well as the tour guides, the general guide to

Manchester has obviously been brought up-to-date too, so, for the second time, welcome to Morrissey's Manchester and welcome to my Manchester too!

Phill Gatenby,
May 2009.

PRE-VISIT APPETISERS

Recommended books and films to view before you arrive to get you into the Manchester Mood:

BOOKS

MANCHESTER, ENGLAND - THE STORY OF THE POP CULT CITY
Dave Haslam (Fourth Estate 1999)

This book takes you right back in time to the beginnings of Manchester - its history, politics and popular culture - and takes you all the way through to the present day. In between is an account of how the city became renowned the world over for producing talented musicians time and again. It also includes many references to The Smiths / Morrissey. A serious and exhaustive account that somehow manages not to miss a thing.

I SWEAR I WAS THERE
David Nolan (Milo Books 2001)

An account of The Sex Pistols first gig in Manchester in June 1976. The subsequent effect this event had on those present was astonishing - most of the audience went on to become a musical force throughout the 80s and 90s themselves. Sadly, it doesn't feature an interview with Morrissey – who was there – but there are references to him. Definitely one for the old (and new) punks who refuse to die!

THE NORTH WILL RISE AGAIN: MANCHESTER MUSIC 1978 - 2008
(Aurum Press Ltd 2009)

The book details Manchester's punk, post punk, Madchester and present day scenes and tells the stories of a number of the city's most famous musicians. Morrissey, Ian Brown, Noel and Liam Gallagher and The Fall frontman Mark E Smith are among the contributors to the book, alongside Johnny Marr, Happy Mondays frontman Shaun Ryder and the late Factory Records boss Tony Wilson.

ADVENTURES ON THE WHEELS OF STEEL
by Dave Haslam (Fourth Estate 2001)

Haslam takes you around Britain to bring you the atmosphere of clubs far and wide. Includes a chapter titled 'A Night At The Anti Disco Disco' - an account of a Smiths & Morrissey Night at the Star and Garter, Manchester - and a chapter on the farewell party for The Hacienda (see the film Twenty Four Hour Party People below). A unique peek into the minds of DJs, promoters and punters and the venues at which they appear.

FILMS

A TASTE OF HONEY (1961)

Adapted from the 1958 play of the same title and filmed in black & white, Shelagh Delaney's classic 'Kitchen Sink Drama', tells the story of a teenage Salford girl (played by the debutant Rita Tushingham) that caused quite a stir when released due to the subject matter of teenage pregnacy, interracial relationships and homosexuality.

Filmed on location in Manchester, Salford and Stockport, very few areas of the film are recognisable today - one notable exception being the ballroom scene which was filmed at The Ritz - the venue of The Smiths debut gig some twenty-one years later.

The play/film clearly had an influence on the young Morrissey as many of the lines were 'borrowed' and used in songs such as 'Reel Around The Fountain', 'These Things Take Time' and 'This Night Has Opened My Eyes'. Delaney's photo appeared on the album cover artwork for The Smiths compilation 'Louder Than Bombs' as well as a different picture for the cover for the bands single "Girlfriend In A Coma".

Coincidently, extracts featuring Tushingham from a later film 'The Leather Boys' was superimposed behind Morrissey singing, and used for the promotional video to the same song.

THERE'S ONLY ONE JIMMY GRIMBLE (2000)

Shot entirely on location around Manchester (Ancoats,

Hulme, Moss Side) this film has a cracking soundtrack (Charlatans, Stone Roses, Echo & the Bunnymen) and also features a young girl who hangs around the local cemetery reading gravestones! There is also a scene at a pub on the way to a football game, with the Star and Garter (venue for the Smiths and Morrissey nights) the boozer in question. Recommended.

THE PAROLE OFFICER (2001)

Filmed extensively around the city centre along with short sequences shot on Blackpool Pleasure Beach, Liverpool and Saddleworth Moor. A hapless probation officer (British name for a parole officer) is framed for a murder that he witnessed and recruits a gang of ex-prisoners he has helped to go straight so he can prove his innocence - only this involves breaking into a bank to retrieve vital evidence! Can they pull it off? Plenty of laughs guaranteed.

TWENTY FOUR HOUR PARTY PEOPLE (2002)

This (semi-fictional) film charts the rise and fall of the world famous Hacienda Club and Factory Records. Naturally, you can be guaranteed a great soundtrack to accompany this film. The club scenes were filmed in an old warehouse in Ancoats as the Hacienda was recreated for a final farewell party, covered by Hacienda DJ Dave Haslam in his book Adventures on the Wheels of Steel (see books above).

ARRIVING AND SURVIVING IN MANCHESTER

ARRIVING IN MANCHESTER

It has never been easier to travel to Manchester.

By air: Manchester Airport is the biggest in the UK outside of London. Trains run frequently throughout the day (and less frequently during the night) from the airport right into the heart of the city.

By train: Manchester has two main stations (Piccadilly and Victoria), trains arriving from all directions of the country.

By coach: Again, Manchester is a main destination from all routes to its Manchester Central (formerly Chorlton Street) Bus Station right in the middle of the city centre.

By ferry: access to trains is easy from the following ports - Holyhead, Liverpool and Heysham.

By car: the opening of the complete Manchester Orbital link road (M60) in 2000 provided the region with easy access to all roads north, south, east and west.

From London and the south east: follow the M1, M6, M56.

From the east: follow the M62 (north east - follow A1M, M62).

From the north west and Scotland: follow the M6 and M61.

From the south west /South Wales: follow (M4, M50) M5, M6, M56.

From North Wales: M56.

PUBLIC TRANSPORT WITHIN MANCHESTER

For the purpose of travelling to and from the places highlighted in the tour, in most cases this involves catching a bus or Metrolink tram.

For buses, you do not need the exact fare, change will be given, but it will help if you have smaller change handy rather than large notes. Most buses depart from Piccadilly Gardens. However, because of the re-development of the Gardens, this means that some buses now depart from the streets immediately surrounding them.

There are regular information boards on bus stops indicating which location each bus now departs from. If in doubt, ask a driver!

To add to the confusion, there are also different bus companies operating in the same area and day tickets from one company may not be transferable to use on a bus from a different company. You need to ask for a daily bus ticket that enables you to travel on *any* bus in Greater Manchester (a System One ticket) and if you are going on the Metrolink (see below) ask for that to be included on the ticket too.

If you are staying for more than a few days, ask about daily or weekly passes at the Travel Shop on Piccadilly gardens.

Metrolink trams run through the city centre very regularly, with each destination clearly positioned on the front of each tram. Payment for tickets must be done at the platform ticket machine before you embark on your journey. There are no ticket barriers, but regular spot checks are carried out by inspectors and passengers caught travelling without tickets face an on the spot fine of up £80. You have been warned!

*Please note both buses and trams run a reduced service in the evenings, Sundays and Public holidays.

For local bus and train enquires call (0161) 228 7811

For Metrolink enquiries call (0161) 205 2000

TAXIS

Taxis come in two forms; the traditional black Hackney carriage and the private hire cars. You can flag down a black cab anywhere and commence your journey. Private hire cars cannot be flagged down and must be ordered in advance.

Private hire cars are regular cars but with illuminated stickers on the sides and bonnet and a licence plate on the back. Do not get into a taxi you haven't ordered, no matter where you are or what state you are in! If a car pulls up claiming to be a taxi and offering you a lift, refuse to get in. You are not insured if you haven't ordered it and it may not be a genuine licensed hire car.

KEEPING IN TOUCH WITH HOME

In these days of electronic communication, it has never been so easy to stay in touch with relatives and friends back home while travelling.

Payphones are situated all over the city centre and take both coins (minimum call 40p) and phone cards. There are Post Offices situated on Spring Gardens and Brazennose Street. Most hotels have internet access available.

SURVIVING IN MANCHESTER

This section states the obvious, but sometimes the obvious needs stating. As with any visitor to any large city, there are dangers lurking around every corner that can be avoided if the following is adhered to:

ACCOMMODATION

Book your accommodation before arriving in Manchester and go to your hotel straight away, do not walk around the city centre looking for banks and shops while carrying your bags. Blend in and look local! Plan your route before leaving your room, so as not to appear hopelessly lost in an area where you might be taken advantage of.

The following hotels are based in the city centre (indeed throughout the UK), some with more than one site available:

The Ibis Hotel - www.ibishotels.com
Jurys Inn - www.jurysdoyle.com
The Novotel - www.novotel.com
Premier Lodge - www.premierlodge.com

Travel Inn Metro - www.travelinn.co.uk
Further accommodation can be found at:
www.destinationmanchester.com

There are plenty of rooms available throughout the city but they do get booked up when there is a European or domestic match or a big concert in the city, so book early!

PERSONAL SAFETY

Morrissey's Manchester tours do lead you into some areas where care should be taken at all times. I suggest you start as early as you can, allowing plenty of time to complete whichever tour you choose before the late afternoon. Remember, in the winter it starts to go dark around 4pm. If possible, do not travel alone, however, do not travel in too large a number either! The appearance of a 'gang' descending on certain districts will attract unwanted curiosity amongst local youths.

Do not draw attention to yourself, no matter how excited you are about standing in front of The Salford Lads Club or Morrissey's house in Kings Road, just take the picture and move on.

Do not take with you on the tour large amounts of money and expensive cameras etc. Currently, you do not need to carry identification on you in Britain, so leave your passport in the hotel.

Stick to the main roads while in the city centre and suburbs, again, planning your route in advance.

In addition, there are a lot of aggressive beggars in the city centre. They tend to hang around bus or train stations, looking desperate as they inform you that they have lost their ticket and desperately need to get back to a given destination immediately and can you spare them any money to help them! Tourists are likely to be targeted, but be polite and walk past them and they will not bother you. Keep your eye on your bags and belongings when in bars, restaurants or on public transport. And be aware when getting on to public transport, it can be a pick pocket's heaven!

DRUGS

Everyone has an opinion as to which drugs should be legalised and which shouldn't be. This is not the forum to debate the issue. The fact remains, however, that the following drugs are, at the time of writing, illegal in Britain: soft drugs such as cannabis, ecstasy, amphetamines and unprescribed barbiturates. Hard drugs including heroin, magic mushrooms, LSD, cocaine and crack.

Should you have any issue with drugs while in Manchester, an agency called 'Lifeline' is situated at 101-103 Oldham Street and is open throughout the day time and can be telephoned on (0161) 839 2054.

EMERGENCY SERVICES

For the police, ambulance and fire brigade call 999 for emergencies only. This can be done for free from any public payphone. For non-emergency calls to the police, call (0161) 872 5050.

CHEMISTS

There is a city centre chemist that opens until midnight every night - Cameolord, St Peters Square, 7 Oxford Street.

OFFENSIVE WEAPONS

It is an offence to carry knives, CS gas sprays and guns in Britain. Even in self-defence these weapons are illegal.

LOCAL INFORMATION

The Manchester Visitor Information Centre is situated in The Town Hall Extension, Lloyd Street in the city centre. Call (0161) 236 9900

www.manchester.gov.uk/visitorcentre

The *Manchester Evening News* is published daily Monday - Saturday with a daily entertainment guide (and an excellent weekend supplement on a Friday) The MEN is given out free throughout the city centre Monday - Fridays.

www.manchesteronline.co.uk

Metro News is a free morning newspaper distributed throughout the city centre, Monday to Friday and available on public transport and stations, hotels and at other public venues. An extensive listing is given to the day's entertainment catering for all tastes.

www.metro.co.uk

The Big Issue is another publication you will find for sale on the streets. Packed with issue based news that escapes the national papers and local reviews, the weekly magazine is sold by homeless people with the aim of helping them to get off the streets. The vendors keep a percentage of the sales of each copy sold.

<u>www.bigissueinthenorth.com</u>

BANKS

There are plenty of banks within the city centre, mostly centred around Spring Gardens, Piccadilly and the universities. They are open from 9.30am until 3.30pm, but some remain open until 4.30pm. If you need to withdraw money from a bank, use the counter inside rather than the cash machine in the wall outside. Think ahead and withdraw cash in the day rather than using the cash points in the evening.

TIPPING

We British have a different culture of tipping than most other countries. Or to put it another way, we generally do not tip! A few exceptions include in restaurants or occasionally in a taxi if the driver isn't too miserable! Some restaurants add a service charge to the bill (check the menu first), some do not and it is up to your discretion as to how much you leave.

THE WEATHER

Yes the rain does fall hard on a hum drum town, but not as much as claimed by protagonists! Manchester does have a lot of rain, but not in quantity, just with more regularity! So, while the summers can be reasonably warm, but certainly dry, it is best to pack that rain coat just in case no matter what time of year you are visiting.

Certainly in winter, make sure you bring those warm clothes with you! Besides, it wouldn't be the same if you visited Manchester and it didn't rain, now would it?!

FINALLY...

If you are visiting from outside the UK, we drive on the left-hand side of the road. Please bear this in mind when crossing the road and specifically if you are driving a car!

Seriously, all of the above is aimed at maximising your safety to give you as enjoyable time as possible. Please remember Manchester is no better or worse than any other major city in terms of personal safety. By being fully alert at all times and preparing your trip effectively you should ensure that your visit to this great city is safe and pleasant.

Indeed, I hope Manchester is a trip to remember, a place to return to and a destination to recommend to others.

TEN MINUTE MANCHESTER

There are plenty of books to read if you are particularly interested in Manchester's past. There are lots of bookshops around the city centre as well as the Tourist Information Shop or you could visit the Local Studies Unit at the city's huge Central Library, on St Peter's Square (situated next to the Tourist Information Shop).

I certainly do not wish to write an epic script on the history of the city in these pages, but feel the guide should have some historical input, listing the key events that shaped this great city.

THE FIRST INHABITANTS

The Roman invasion of Britain brought the first residents of Manchester. In around AD70 a fort and settlement was built at the point where the River Medlock flows into the River Irwell.

The original Roman name of Manchester was Mamucium (later Mancunium), as the fort was situated on 'a breast like hill'. Yes, Manchester was named after a big tit!

The settlement was situated on the road between Chester (Deva) and York (Eboracum). Today, this site

- known as Castlefield - has been preserved, indeed it become Britain's first Urban Heritage Park, complete with mock fort, a visitors centre and a small Roman amphitheatre, which regularly hosts carnivals and free gigs during the warmer months of the year.

MEDIEVAL MANCHESTER

During the medieval period (1100-1400), the residents had moved further upstream along The Irwell, at its junction with the River Irk, (where the Cathedral currently stands). Manchester remained just a small market town in the south of the county of Lancashire with an annual fair, it had little importance in terms of commerce or wealth.

THE WORLD'S FIRST MODERN CITY

Manchester had quietly developed over the centuries, gradually becoming a wealthy (and therefore powerful) district. By the late 1700s, almost 75% of Britain's cotton industry was centred around Manchester and its surrounding districts, the reason being that good old Manchester weather - the rain!

The dampness, coupled with the soft Pennine hill waters, made ideal conditions in which to spin cotton. Then, as transport improved, firstly the canals, followed by the railways, allowed for trade to develop and expand further. As more and more mills were built, Manchester became known as 'Cottonopolis' producing textiles that travelled the globe. Soon everyone wanted to see Manchester's blueprint for success and many took the idea of an industrial city and implemented similar models in towns and cities around the world.

THE PETERLOO MASSACRE.

This particular chapter in Manchester's story is perhaps the most important of all. Hand in hand with the burgeoning industrial revolution came a growing need for workers rights and trade unionism. Manchester became feared in London for its radicalism and political leaders. Public meetings were regularly held, many turning into protests, frequently leading to riots. Those convicted of rioting were hanged, as magistrates fought hard to maintain civil order. Eventually, the government banned all forms of public meetings in 1817.

However, this did not prevent meetings from taking place and on that fateful day - 16th August 1819 - thousands of men, women and children marched from Manchester's neighbouring towns into St Peter's Fields demanding 'More Rights For Man'.

The sheer size of the demonstration worried local magistrates. At this time there was no police force in England, so the local Manchester Yeomanry (volunteer soldiers) and the 15th Hussars were called up to disperse the crowd. The magistrates called for the arrest of the organisers and speakers of the meeting and sent in the Yeomen to make arrests.

However, while making their way back through the crowd with their detainees, the Yeoman panicked and indiscriminately lashed out with their swords and havoc ensued. The Hussars were sent in on horseback to disperse the public and by the time it was all over, eleven people had died and another six hundred were injured.

Outbreaks of violence took place over the next few days in several districts against the cavalry and attacks were made on the businesses of the Yeomanry. The tragic event was given the name 'The Peterloo Massacre' as the 15th Hussars had, four years before, been in action at the Battle of Waterloo.

TRAINSPOTTING

The world's first trainspotter may well have been present at Liverpool Road Station, Manchester on 15th September 1830 as the world's first passenger-carrying steam train left the station destined for Liverpool.

THE ANTI-CORN LEAGUE

In 1815, the Government had introduced 'The Corn Law'. This act decreed that a duty be levied on the importation of corn from abroad with the aim, it was said, to maintain the price of corn sold by British producers. However, it soon came to be seen as a tax to ensure that landowners maintained their profits.

Emboldened by the success of the Chartists and Trade Union movements, The Anti-Corn Law Association was formed in Manchester in 1838, with the aim of declaring 'Free Trade Between Nations'.

Once more, it was through public meetings that support for the campaign grew and significantly in 1840 a building was constructed in Manchester to host such meetings.

The original timber 'Free Trade' building took just six weeks to complete and poignantly was situated on the exact spot of The Peterloo Massacre.

The Free Trade Hall has been rebuilt twice - in 1843 and 1853 - but it still remains today - just about - on Peter Street. (See 'Free Trade Hall' on City Centre Tour)

The historian AJP Taylor remarked 'Other great halls in England are called after a royal patron or some figure of traditional religion. Only The Free Trade Hall is dedicated to a proposition.'

During the 1840s the campaigners certainly had the increased support of public opinion and the act was finally repealed by Parliament in 1846. However, this was not seen as a victory for the campaigners as the seriousness of the 'Great Famine' in Ireland forced the Prime Minister to take action that ensured food from abroad could be imported cheaply to feed the nation.

A CITY AT LAST!

Manchester was granted City status (becoming the second city of the Empire) by Queen Victoria in 1853.

THE MANCHESTER MARTYRS

The 1800s saw the bitter struggle continue in Ireland between The Irish Republican Brotherhood (The Fenians) and the British army. During the latter part of the century, the cause of the republicans was carried out on English soil. Frequent strikes on railway stations and gas works amongst other public places became common occurrences.

In 1867 two suspected Fenian leaders were arrested in Manchester and a few days later they were transferred to Belle Vue Gaol. However, on their way down Hyde Road, the horse drawn vehicle was attacked by a large mob of Fenian supporters. The two prisoners escaped but a policeman was shot and killed during the raid. As a result twenty-eight men were arrested and charged with the murder of the policeman.

During the November trial, five were found guilty of the murder, three of whom were publicly hanged in Salford Gaol. It is commonly believed that the bodies of the Martyrs are buried beneath a memorial monument in St Joseph's cemetery in Moston. However, the authorities have never released the bodies of the three. They were initially buried in the grounds of the New Bailey prison in Salford after they were executed. About two years later, when that building was demolished, their remains were re-interred in the grounds of the newly built Strangeways jail. There they remained until 1991 when, following the Strangeways riots, the prison was re-developed and the remains of the three were removed to Blackley cemetery in north Manchester. There is currently a campaign to have the remains returned to Ireland.

The following years saw more disturbances and riots, with an infamous meeting taking place on one particular day in 1868 in a field in Chorlton. The meeting was a show of anti-Catholic feeling in Manchester. The meeting included the bizarre scene of the six thousand strong crowd giving: 'Three cheers for the Queen, another three for William, Prince of Orange and three boos for the Pope!'

GIRL POWER

Manchester again continued to be at the forefront of radical thinking and for the first time it was women leading the way. Lydia Becker formed 'The National Society For Women's Suffrage' in 1867, after an updated act of Parliament failed to allow women the right to vote.

Becker (born in Manchester in 1827) became the first woman to address a public meeting, which was also the first meeting in the country to discuss women's suffrage. And at which venue did the meeting take place in? The Free Trade Hall, of course! Becker continued with her role with the society, until her death in 1890.

However another group that later became known as 'The Suffragette Movement', was also formed in Manchester. While sharing the same aims as Becker's gentile society, the suffragettes placed greater stress on direct action to further their cause. Their founder Emmeline Pankhurst was born in Manchester in 1858 and with the help of her two daughters, she formed the 'Women's Social and Political Union' (WSPU) at her home in Manchester in 1903. Members of the WPSU were subsequently arrested and jailed for smashing windows and committing arson.

A young Winston Churchill was addressing one meeting in the Free Trade Hall when two women, Emmeline's daughter Christabel and her friend Annie

Kenney, disrupted the meeting, demanding voting rights for women.

Ignoring requests to be silent, Kenney spat at a policemen who was about to eject the pair. She was subsequently sentenced to seven days in Strangeways Prison. Others imprisoned embarked on a series of hunger strikes and were brutally force-fed by prison wardens.

It was this militancy that split public opinion and it is perceived that the arguments of the Society won the day rather than the antics of the suffragettes. In 1918 women over thirty were allowed to vote, with those over twenty-one achieving the same rights as men in 1928.

Today there is a museum dedicated to the Suffragette Movement at Emmeline Pankhurst's former home in Nelson Street, near Manchester University and in 2008, three high rise apartment blocks in Collyhurst were gutted, redeveloped and given the individual names of Emmeline, Sylvia and Christabel in tribute.

ALBERT SQUARE, MANCHESTER TOWN HALL

The city leaders, wishing to show the world how grand and self confident Manchester had become, set aside £1m to build a large, imposing, gothic structure complete with a great tower housing a clock. On top of the tower, a golden cotton seed sits proudly as a tribute to the wealth it has given the city.

After seven years in the making, the Town Hall, designed by Alfred Waterhouse (who went on to design London's Natural History Museum) opened in

1887 and remains to this day as Manchester's main civic building. The square was named after Queen Victoria's late husband, Albert - whose statue is prominent at the front of the square.

MANCHESTER-BY-THE-SEA

Manchester's movers and shakers of the late 19th Century felt that the city could offer more to the world but was being held back by its location 35 miles from the Irish Sea. They were also becoming increasingly frustrated at the rising charges set by both the Port of Liverpool and the rail companies for handling and carriage of goods.

As a result it was decided that as Manchester couldn't move to the sea, it would bring the sea to Manchester! While this seemed highly unlikely geographically, it was, in fact, an ideal opportunity. For, although Manchester was surrounded by the Pennine Hills to the north, east and south, to the west lay the open, flat, Cheshire plains leading from the city straight through to the Mersey estuary, which led directly into the Irish Sea and beyond. The aim was quickly established to bypass Liverpool altogether.

The newly formed Manchester Ship Canal Company commenced the massive task of constructing the vast channel, 35 miles long and cut as deep as the Suez Canal, with labour provided by thousands of Irish immigrants, known as 'Navvies'. Many of these men subsequently stayed to work on the docks and distribution centres in the giant Trafford Park Industrial Estate that grew alongside the canal.

The canal was completed in a remarkable seven years between 1887 to 1894. Yet, not surprisingly, the Ship Canal Company ran out of funds part way through and had to be rescued by Manchester City Corporation, in a deal that gave the council a powerful position on the board of the company.

However the world's biggest liners could now sail right into Manchester, much to the annoyance of their Lancashire cousins in Liverpool as a slump in trade hit their economy hard. Liverpool never forgave Manchester for building the canal and the intense political (as well as musical and sporting) rivalry between the cities remains to this day.

Nevertheless, the canal is a fantastic feat of engineering. Just as it enters the docks in Manchester, vessels pass through the splendidly constructed Barton Aqueduct and the 'Barton Swing Bridge' as it is known locally. This unique aqueduct - the only type of its kind in the world - actually carries the Bridgewater Canal above the Ship Canal and was the first aqueduct contructed anywhere in the world since Roman times. The impact the canal had on Manchester was immense and for decades the port remained one of the busiest in Britain. Not bad, for a city 35 miles from the sea!

SCIENCE AND ENGINEERING

If the canal demonstrated Manchester's influence on the industrial revolution, the 1904 meeting of Messrs Rolls and Royce in Hulme was surely the apogee of consumerism. Their world-famous cars have become the ultimate status symbols of the modern age.

Later, during World War Two, Alan Turing, working at Manchester University, produced a device able to crack the Enigma code used by the German Navy that helped the allies win the Battle of the Atlantic.

In 1948 Turing supervised the construction of the ACE, the Automatic Computing Engine, the world's first programmable computer. A brilliant mathematician, Turing tragically killed himself by eating a poisoned apple in 1954 (an event depicted in the eponymous electronics manufacturer's logo) aged just 42, after he was prosecuted for homosexuality and then forced to undergo clinical treatment for a 'cure'.

Only in recent years has his contribution been acknowledged with a statue in Sackville Park, ideally situated between UMIST (University of Manchester Institute of Science & Technology) and the Gay Village. A section of the city's outer ring road has subsequently been named 'Alan Turing Way'.

GREATER MANCHESTER

In 1974 Manchester and its surrounding towns were taken out of the county of Lancashire to become Greater Manchester County. However, the county, along with other metropolitan districts formed at the time, did not last 20 years. In the late 1980s Margaret Thatcher took revenge on them for being too left wing and troublesome, and dissolved their power, handing it over to local district authority.

The county now exists in name only and areas such as the city of Manchester govern themselves.

THATCHER'S BRITAIN

Manchester, along with most northern cities in the 1980s, suffered under the right-wing government of Margaret Thatcher. The decaying backdrop for many of The Smiths and Morrissey's finest work, Manchester was a grim place during the 1970s and 1980s as long-standing industries were finally shut down and unemployment rose to record levels.

However, the late 1980s saw a resurgence. Determined to restore the city's international image the council launched a series of initiatives to clean up the city before launching an ambitious, if unsuccessful bid for the 1996 and 2000 Olympic Games and, finally, a successful bid for the 2002 Commonwelath Games.

CITY CENTRE REDEVELOPMENT

In 1996, the IRA exploded their biggest bomb ever on the British mainland on Corporation Street. Amazingly, nobody was killed, although some were injured and more were traumatised. From such negativity, a positive outlook was taken and the city defiantly fought back to rebuild the area in typical Mancunian style. Indeed many believe the IRA did us a favour by exploding the bomb outside one of the biggest eyesores in the city!

Clearly, Manchester is a confident, forward-thinking and progressive place. It has been said that 'what Manchester does today the world does tomorrow' and it has never been truer than the present day:

'Manchester, so much to be thankful for..'

MANCHESTER TODAY

'I came back to my old city... and I couldn't find my way back to the station, it's all changed'

So complained Morrissey on 'Heir Apparent' and it's not surprising as the city centre has undergone such a transformation since Morrissey's move to America's west coast. Even Piccadilly Station - as the song states - has succumbed to development. The Piccadilly Approach road at the front being switched to the new Fairfield Road entrance at the rear for cars and taxis.

Manchester is a mixture of the old and new, the old is often beautiful, the new often a monstrosity. Take for example, Beetham Tower. Located along Deansgate at the junction with Great Bridgewater Street and Liverpool Road, it has 47 floors and is nearly 169 metres high, making it the tallest building in the UK outside of London and the tallest residential development in Europe. On a clear day, you can see the Welsh mountains, both Liverpool Cathedrals and the Blackpool Tower! However, the building is so out of place with its surroundings and its 'straight up lego style' design has not won over local hearts.

The city centre has undergone a huge change over

the last fifteen years. Many of the old warehouses, having been left derelict for decades have now been converted into luxury apartments for the trendy and upwardly mobile.

New hotels, coffee bars and street cafes have opened up all over the city centre. After the IRA bomb in 1996, new shopping areas were built from the ashes and it would appear that the city planners are finally getting things right following the awful 1960s and 1970s when they built dreadful eyesores (see the Arndale Centre on Market Street as a fine example).

Adding to the throng on the street at this time is the biggest student population in Europe. Over 40,000 students attend the four universities in the area each year.

Manchester is also a cosmopolitan city; the industrial revolution brought migrants from many countries who settled here. We have a big Irish population and the largest Chinese and Jewish communities outside London, alongside Polish, Italian and lots of other established communities as well.

Over the last 50 years, Asian and Afro-Caribbean people have settled and contributed to the city's success. However, it must be said that most of these communities have settled around the south and south-east of the city centre (Hulme, Moss Side, Rusholme, Whalley Range, Old Trafford, Fallowfield, Longsight, Levenshulme). To the east and north of the city centre, the districts of Ardwick, Beswick, Clayton, Openshaw, Gorton, Newton Heath, Miles Platting, Moston, Harpurhey, Collyhurst and Blackley remain predominantly white, working-class areas of red-bricked terraced housing. The only exception is Cheetham Hill, in the north-west corner of the city, with a pocket of a large Asian population bordered by the district of Prestwich, officially in the Borough of Bury, home to the city's large Jewish community.

Mirroring the north-south divide of England, there is a definite north-south divide in Manchester. The south side attracts the largest house prices, receives better public transport, has the universities, leisure, sport, entertainment and eateries on their doorstep. Those living in the north and east of the city have to travel into the city centre or into the south side to receive the same services, although this is changing.

And to the west of Manchester? Well, Manchester has no west! Through the city centre the River Irwell flows and anything west of the river is in the City of Salford.

To Mancunians, Salford is an extension of the city and anything successful from Salford is Mancunian success too. Yet Salfordians will rightly and proudly proclaim that Salford is a city in its own right and often complain about sharing the 'M' postcode and the '0161' telephone dialling code. 'Salford belongs to Lancashire and not Manchester' is the regular complaint.

There's little doubt that Salford has been enveloped by its big brother and few Mancunians could give you a reason for visiting it (apart from the Salford Lads Club!). In the last couple of years however, a few developments have raised the area's profile. The most significant being the construction of the Lowry art gallery and the opening of the new Media City complex in 2011 in Salford Quays as well as the opening of the first 5 star hotel in the area for years.

Manchester also has a thriving gay scene. The area around Sackville Street has had a reputation for being a homosexual haunt since the 1930s. During the mid 1980s this developed into a few gay bars and clubs in the run down part of the city centre around Chorlton Street bus station. Then, one by one, the buildings in the area were developed and more gay clubs opened.

Later, gay-owned businesses and shops were followed by restaurants, apartments and the so-called 'Pink Pound' became a powerful influence on the city.

The development centred around Canal Street catapulted the area to prominence and a vibrant scene quickly established an international reputation. The Gay Village (as it was called) actually became the safest area in the city centre, to such an extent that the heteros started flocking there because trouble caused at other clubs made them unsafe to visit.

Straight women in particular would visit the Gay Village as it was a haven for them without the hassle of guys trying to hit on them all night. But then straight males became wise to the situation and followed suit. The hit TV show Queer as Folk, with extensive filming on Canal Street, also popularised the area attracting voyeurs down to have a look.

This has resulted in some gay people boycotting

the Village (as it is now called – the 'Gay' having been dropped by a media still too uncomfortable with the tag!) claiming it is too straight and they get hassle from straight males who go down to stare at the inhabitants of the area as if they were in a zoo.

As a result, the clubs that previously let in 'gay friendly' people, are now either exclusively gay or heteros have to be accompanied by gay friends. Unfortunately the area has become a victim of its own success.

Festivals that take place regularly include the Chinese New Year celebrations in February, the Irish Festival around St Patrick's Day, St. George's Day Parade, the Lord Mayor's Parade, the German Christmas Markets, the Italian Festival, Whit Walks Parades and Manchester Pride. A full and updated list can be found on Manchester City Council's website:

www.manchester.gov.uk

MANCHESTER TOURS

These tours are split into four sections and are designed to be taken on foot. Each section can be visited in any order appropriate to the time you have available and preferences of places to visit. In all sections, places of interest are close by to one another.

Since the publication of my book 'Morrissey's Manchester' in 2002, Morrissey has performed in Manchester (including neighbouring Salford and Trafford) on ten occasions, in five new venues and five other places of interest have also been included in this edition.

Manchester itself was name checked twice during songs of The Smiths: 'The Headmaster Ritual' declares 'Belligerent Ghouls run Manchester schools' whilst 'Suffer Little Children' states 'Oh Manchester, so much to answer for'. There was also a version of 'This Charming Man' - The Manchester Mix (which was actually recorded at Strawberry Studios in Stockport, some seven miles south east of the city).

PICCADILLY PALARE?

The best starting point for the tour is in the heart of

the city centre at Piccadilly Gardens. However, this is not the 'Piccadilly' referred to in Morrissey's song 'Piccadilly Palare', but the Piccadilly in London.

SECTION 1 – THE CITY CENTRE

From the gardens, the first port of call is halfway down Portland Street on the right hand side of the road, around the corner from Piccadilly Hotel.

CRAZY FACE 1, 70 PORTLAND STREET

Directions: Walking down Portland Street on the right hand side, to the junction of Nicholas Street on the edge of China Town. The building on the opposite side of the junction is number 70 and is currently a beauty parlour called 'Nail City', with a basement Thai restaurant called 'Red Chilli'. Fortunately, this block on Portland Street remains one of the few that has been left unscathed from demolition and redevelopment over the last decade and a half.

Reference: In 1982, this building was Crazy Face Wholesale Clothing Co. Ltd, one of a small chain of businesses owned by Joe Moss, The Smiths first manager. Moss took advantage of the space available in the building and offered the fledgling band a room upstairs to rehearse in.

Clearly a venue of importance for the band in their early days, where they practised together, experimenting and creating the sound that later became their own.

THE MANHATTAN, 60 SPRING GARDENS

Directions: Walk the length of Nicholas Street, through China Town, over the tramlines on Mosley Street onto Booth Street and take the second right onto Fountain Street. The first road on your left is Spring Gardens and the first building on your left is number 60.

In the seventies and early eighties The Manhattan

was a basement club, offering food as well as entertainment. The whole building was demolished in 1985 and re-opened a year later. This area is in the heart of the financial and legal district and the building now belongs to an insurance company.

Reference: Gig – 6th January 1983

Additional information: In the seventies and early eighties, this was the site of The Manhattan, a basement club and venue for The Smiths second gig on 6th January 1983 supporting 'Foreign Press'. Andy Rourke had now joined the band since their first gig (see The Ritz) and this was his live debut as a member of the band. After the gig, it was decided that the band's 'dancer' James Maker (see The Ritz), was more of a distraction than an attraction and his stint in the band came to an end.

CRAZY FACE 2 AND X CLOTHES, CHAPEL WALKS

Directions: Follow Spring Gardens on the left hand

side and turn third left into King Street. Cross over immediately and take the first right which is Brown Street. Turn into Marsden Street which is the first left and continue down Marsden Street which becomes Chapel Walks as the street narrows and is only for pedestrians. As the two merge, on your right is 'Buccanillio', a Mediterranean restaurant.

Reference: In the early 80's, the building was two separate clothing outlets. Joe Moss owned the shop Crazy Face and Johnny Marr worked next door in X Clothes. It was here that the pair first met, becoming close friends and sharing influences. Without a doubt, the first seed of The Smiths were sown on Chapel Walks and had the pair not met it is questionable as to whether the band would have formed.

FREE TRADE HALL, PETER STREET

Directions: Continue down Chapel Walks to the end, turning left onto Cross Street and going over the lights at King Street. At the next lights you are on the edge of the Town Hall and Albert Square. Cross over and across the square, heading for the right hand corner to Southmill Street. Continue down Southmill Street until you reach the junction with Peter Street. The site of the Free Trade Hall is on the opposite side of the road on your right – now the Radisson Hotel.

This was Manchester's most important historical building and it is to the council's discredit that it no longer remains intact on this site. Originally built as a timber structure in 1840, it was rebuilt three years later, this time with bricks. A further ten years later it was rebuilt again, this time using stone.

The site chosen for the building was symbolic of 'The Peterloo Massacre' that took place at St Peter's Fields on Sunday 16th August 1819 (see p. 16).

Many concerts took place in the hall, including a famous show by Bob Dylan, when he picked up his electric guitar and a member of the audience shouted 'Judas' at the singer. This was captured on a bootleg, though incorrectly titled 'Live at The Royal Albert Hall' and also featured in a famous 1966 film 'Don't Look Back' made by documentary maker DA Pennebaker.

The Sex Pistols also performed their first gig outside London on 4th June 1976 in an upstairs theatre known as The Lesser Free Trade Hall. The Pistols had been invited to perform by Pete Shelley and Howard Devoto who also formed the Buzzcocks. This truly was a 'life changing' concert, at least as far as Manchester's music scene is concerned, as amongst the small audience that night were Morrissey, Bernard Sumner and Peter Hook (Joy Division, New Order), Mark E Smith (The Fall), Mick Hucknall (Frantic Elevators, Simply Red), Tony Wilson (Granada TV and Factory Records), Paul Morley (journalist and co founder of ZTT Records), Linder Sterling (Ludas) and John The Postman! John became a legendary figure amongst the Manchester punk scene by jumping on stage between acts, grabbing the microphone and giving an impromptu performance of 'Louis Louis'. This whole scene is captured perfectly in Dave Nolan's book, 'I Swear I Was There' and in film in Twenty Four Hour Party People.

The Halle Orchestra were the hall's permanent

tenants for decades until the late 1990s but sought a new purpose built home. When they moved out into The Bridgewater Hall (see Bridgewater Hall) in 1996, the hall was closed, boarded up and gradually became un-repairable. The site was sold to developers who

wanted to build a 5 star hotel on top of the hall. In 2002 demolition started and the hotel opened in 2005. Only the front facade of the hall remains of a building that shaped the city and its development, helping Manchester to trade with every corner of the world.

Reference: Gigs – The Smiths 13th March 1984, 30th October 1986.

Additional information: The first gig was promoting the self-titled debut album and supported by The Red Guitars.

The second gig was promoting the single 'Ask'. It was Craig Gannon's last appearance in the band as well as it being The Smiths' final hometown performance and – as it turned out – their penultimate live concert. Support came from 'Raymonde', a band featuring James Maker (see The Ritz).

THE OPERA HOUSE, QUAY STREET

Directions: Facing the Free Trade Hall, turn right down Peter Street, crossing over Deansgate and onto Quay Street. The Opera House is a short distance away on the right hand side.

One of Manchester's biggest venues for large theatrical productions, opera, dance and modern West End musicals. This is a very elegant old building, seating 2000.

Initially it was named the 'New Theatre' when it opened on Boxing Day in 1912, 5 years later it changed its name to the 'New Queens'. It took on its present title in the 1930s under new ownership. Suffering a similar fate to many theatres and cinemas, its audiences declined in the 1970s.

Fortunately, in the early 1980s, a renaissance in interest and a great deal of petitioning to save both the Opera House and nearby Palace Theatre (see Palace Theatre) resulted in the Arts Council stepping in and the Opera House being saved and reopened. Now, thanks to a lively and commercial business approach, it is a most successful theatre.

Reference: Gig - Morrissey 7th May 2006

This gig was the second in three consecutive nights at three different venues in Manchester (see Apollo Theatre and Bridgewater Hall) by Morrissey promoting the 'Ringleader Of The Tormentors' album.

Support came from Kristeen Young and Sons & Daughters

GRANADA TV STUDIOS, QUAY STREET

Directions: From the Opera House, the Granada studios are a little further down Quay Street on the opposite side of the road.

Granada TV is north west England's independent television station. It opened in May 1956 - taking its name from the Spanish region of the same name in which the founders of the station (Cecil and Sidney Bernstein) often stayed. Famous for its soap opera 'Coronation Street' it was to these studios where a young Morrissey sent his rejected scripts for the long running series. At the time of writing, Granada are in discussions to sell the site for redevelopment with the aim of moving to a new media centre based on

Salford Quays in 2011 (see also BBC Manchester).

Reference: The studios appear on the back cover of the 1997 reissue of Morrissey's first solo album, 'Viva Hate' that included eight tracks previously only available as early Morrissey b-sides.

THE RIVER IRWELL

Directions: From Granada Studios, continue along Quay Street and the river is two minutes walk.

The original course of the River Irwell is about 39 miles in length, from its source to the confluence with the River Mersey near Irlam. Rising on the moors above Cliviger, the river flows south through Bacup, Rawtenstall, Ramsbottom and Bury. Merging with both the rivers Roch and Croal, it continues through Radcliffe, Kearsley, Clifton and districts of Salford such as Agecroft, Lower Broughton and Kersal and Salford Crescent. In Manchester city centre, the river forms the historic boundary line between Manchester and Salford and takes in the rivers Irk and Medlock too. Once out of the city centre, the river now merges into the Manchester Ship Canal (see page 43), ending the river some ten miles short of its meeting point with the Mersey. The ship canal does follow much of the original course of the Irwell, including passing underneath the unique Barton Swing Bridge at Barton-Upon-Irwell.

The origins of the name 'Irwell' is believed to come from the Anglo-Saxon for 'ere-well', meaning "Hoar or White Spring"

Until the early 19th century the Irwell was well stocked with fish and other wildlife, and people living near Manchester Cathedral used its water for drinking and other domestic purposes. However, during the Industrial Revolution factories, mills and terraced hovels grew up along the river banks. As a result, local industry dumped toxic chemicals into the river, such as gas-tar, gas-lime and ammonia water, and by 1850 fish stocks had all but disappeared.

In 1860 the Irwell was described as "almost proverbial for the foulness of its waters; receiving the refuse of cotton factories, coal mines, print works, bleach works, dye works, chemical works, paper works, almost every kind of industrial waste", prompting this poem, 'The Irwell' by Ronald Y Digby

> *Most rivers have great beauty,*
> *They flow down to the sea ,*
> *With crystal laughing waters,*
> *Reflecting all they see,*
> *But, thou O' River Irwell,*
> *Must wind thy weary way,*
> *Through tunnels, goits and culverts,*
> *With turgid waters grey,*
> *Thou has no purple Kingfishers,*
> *To brighten halcyon days,*
> *No gleaming fish to call thee home,*
> *No jumping trout in May,*
> *Polluted by foul effluents,*
> *For factories a stink,*
> *To living creatures lethal,*
> *Repulsive with thy stink,*

Though country loving aesthetes
From such as thee recoil,
Thou helps to earn a living,
Of countless sons of toil,
Flow on then busy Irwell,
Down to the surging tide,
Thou hardest working river,
In the world - in that they pride

One of the most famous characters associated with the river is Mark Addy, born near to the river at Blackfriars Bridge in Manchester in 1838. Whenever anyone was in difficulty in the river, the cry would go up "Bring Mark Addy!" and he would race to the rescue. He was awarded a number of medals including the gold and silver medals for his bravery and in 1878 he became the only civilian ever to be awarded the Albert Medal (First Class). His final rescue was on Whit Monday in 1889, when he saved a young boy from a particularly sewage-laden section of the river. After this he became ill, and died of tuberculosis in 1890 aged 51. He had rescued over 50 people from the river during his lifetime. On the Salford side of the river off Bridge Street West, there is a pub 'The Mark Addy'.

Beginning in the latter half of the 20th century, a number of initiatives through organisations such as The Mersey Basin Campaign, were implemented to remove the pollution, restock the river with fish and create a diverse environment for wildlife and this has been highly successful though more is still to be achieved. Today, The Irwell is host to a number of recreational activities, such as pleasure cruising, fishing and events such as the annual Two Cities Boat Race, competed for by Manchester and Salford Universities.

Reference: The Smiths song 'This Night Has Opened My Eyes' opens with the lyric 'In a river, the colour of lead...' This is one of several quotes Morrissey 'borrowed' from Shelagh Delaney's play 'A Taste Of Honey' and is a direct reference to The Irwell.

MANCHESTER CENTRAL CONVENTION COMPLEX (FORMERLY G-MEX)

Directions: Return up Quay Street and Peter Street back to the Free Trade Hall, turning right at the end of the hall into Southmill Street, along the side of the hall and the imposing structure of G-Mex is in front of you.

The former Central Station was opened in 1886, serving the towns and villages on the Manchester - Chester line and the last train departed in 1969. Lying derelict for fifteen years the site became the first in Manchester's regeneration of the city centre. Opening in 1986 as the 'Greater Manchester Exhibition Centre'(G-Mex), its 9,000 capacity gave the city a venue to attract the 'stadium rock acts' as the city suffered from the lack of a large indoor venue. Unfortunately, the venue suffered as its cavernous, space was simply too big, having a negative effect on the quality of sound.

Nevertheless, with the absence of any alternative, the big gigs continued and the venue became part of the 'Madchester' culture of the late 80s / early 90s as regular visits became the norm for Happy Mondays, Inspiral Carpets, 808 State and James (whose 'Sit Down' video was filmed here), as well as bands such as U2 and The Pixies.

Eventually, in the mid 90s, Europe's largest indoor arena was built above Victoria train station (see MEN Arena) and the much needed large venue with a quality sound system had arrived, ending the need for G-Mex as a concert venue, leaving it to rely solely on hosting exhibitions, conferences and indoor

funfairs over the Christmas period. Oasis performed the last gig there in 1997. In September 2006 it was announced that G-Mex and its surrounding facilities were to come under the banner of 'Manchester Central Conference Complex' in early 2007.

Yet in a final, bizarre twist, a series of concerts were announced for December 2006 at the venue, with Snow Patrol and Morrissey both performing two nights each.

Reference: Gig – The Smiths 19th July 1986; Morrissey – 22nd, 23rd December 2006.

Additional information: The Smiths performance at G-Mex was part of the 'The Festival Of The Tenth Summer' – a week long festival celebrating the tenth year of the Sex Pistols groundbreaking gig at The Free Trade Hall (see The Free Trade Hall). The final event of the festival was the first concert to be held in the converted train station. Organised by Factory supremo Tony (Anthony, Anthony H) Wilson, the festival climaxed at G-Mex and also in the line up were New Order, The Fall, A Certain Ratio, former members of the Buzzcocks performing under different guises, Sandie Shaw, John Cale, Frank Sidebottom, John Cooper Clarke, OMD as well as a couple of other acts. The Smiths' attendance was in doubt a few weeks before the date, as it was reported that Morrissey was unhappy at the £13 admission charge, claiming it was too expensive. Fortunately, Tony Wilson managed to smooth the issue over and thankfully the band performed at the Festival.

G-Mex was also used for the inside picture cover for The Smiths live album Rank. The picture shows fans ripping apart a shirt thrown into the crowd by Morrissey. Although Rank was actually recorded at Kilburn National Ballroom in London, the shape of the arched former railway station and station clock at the rear are easily identified as G-Mex.

Morrissey's two night stint in 2006 were not only the final shows of that year's huge 'Ringleader Of The Tormentors' tour but also the final concerts ever to be staged at G-Mex, as the venue changed its name in spring 2007, as mentioned above. It appeared to be a quite fitting end – as The Smiths performed at G-Mex's opening concert and Morrissey its final one. Support on both nights came from Kristeen Young.

THE BRIDGEWATER HALL, LOWER MOSLEY STREET

Directions: Facing the front of G-Mex, go left around the side of the former railway station and The Bridgewater Hall is immediately across the road.

The Bridgewater Hall is an international concert venue that cost around £42 million to build and currently hosts over 250 performances a year.

Since its opening on 11 September 1996 it has been the home of the Halle Orchestra and the Manchester Boys' Choir after they vacated The Free

Trade Hall. It is a regular venue for concerts of the BBC Philharmonic and Manchester Camerata. More recently, the venue has hosted performances by artists such as Lou Reed, Van Morrisson, Ray Davies and Nancy Sinatra.

The venue is named 'Bridgewater' after the 3rd Duke of Bridgewater, who commissioned the Bridgewater Canal which crosses Manchester. The canal basin adjacent to the hall is not, however, a branch of the Bridgewater Canal, but of the Rochdale Canal. Inside, the central focal point of the hall is a magnificent pipe organ (with 5,500 pipes) built by Marcussen & Son, which dominates the 2,400 seat auditorium, completely covering the rear wall with a beautiful blend of wood and burnished metal.

The main auditorium sits on a foundation of earthquake-proof isolation bearings (consisting of steel springs) which insulate it from noise and vibration from the adjacent road and Metrolink line.

Reference: Gig – Morrissey May 2006

Additional information: This was the third of three consecutive performances in Manchester at three different venues (see Apollo Theatre and Opera House) promoting the Ringleader Of The Tormentors album. Support came from Tiger Army and Kristeen Young.

THE HACIENDA, WHITWORTH STREET WEST

Directions: Continue past the Bridgewater Hall along Lower Mosley Street, crossing over Great Bridgewater Street and past The Briton's Protection Pub and onto Albion Way. After crossing over the canal, on your

left with the junction of Whitworth Street West is the world famous Hacienda night club – or rather the site of the long gone, but never forgotten Hacienda! What you have now is a block of residential apartments bearing the name of its former historic resident.

The building - with its round frontage - was four stories high with the club on the ground floor and basement. Above it were a number of advertising agencies and other businesses.

The club was a former yacht showroom/warehouse and was bought by Factory Records and opened in 1982 as a night club/concert venue although the sound quality was often poor for live bands. For the first half decade, the club ran at a loss (at the great expense of the four members of New Order whose profits were swallowed up to cover the losses!) and its legendary status only came with the advent of Acid / House Music in the late 80s. The venue instantly became a mecca, attracting sell-out crowds and punters from across the country all flocking to hear the vibes being played by DJs such as Dave Haslam, Mike Pickering (who went on to form M People) and Sasha.

Although Acid and House music are credited with saving the club from extinction, they were also – indirectly – responsible for its downfall. The club's new found profile attracted the attentions of rival inner city gangs from Moss Side, Cheetham Hill and Salford who fought each other over the the right to be the sole supplier to this club and many others operating in the city centre too. Many nights across the city centre were interrupted by fights and occasionally gunfights.

The police came down hard on a number of clubs, objecting to the renewal of their yearly licence to operate with a public entertainment licence and serve alcohol. The Hacienda itself, was closed down in 1991, reopening a few months later - and only when the police were satisfied with new security arrangements put in place.

However it was a few years later when a local magistrate witnessed a violent incident take place outside the club as well as the crippling financial losses due to the previous closure and a fall in attendances forced the club's permanent closure in 1997.

The building remained empty for several years with the exception of a small number of anti capitalist squatters using the venue for a number of demonstrations.

In 2001 the bulldozers moved in and demolished the building. It was hoped that – like The Free Trade

Hall – the round frontage would be preserved and included in the new design, but this was not to be although the shape of the front has been incorporated as a tribute to its past. The interior of the building was carefully dismantled and everything saved and auctioned off with proceeds going to charity – everything from light bulbs, toilet doors, fixtures and fittings, bricks and the famous marble bar.

In 2002, the club was further immortalised with the release of the film 'Twenty-Four Hour Party People', the story of Factory Records. Although the club scenes were filmed in a replica set in a warehouse in Ancoats (your author appears very briefly as an extra, but very clearly on the inside cover of the soundtrack CD!) the closing scene upon the roof (where God appears and tells Anthony Wilson that he should have signed The Smiths!) was filmed on the roof of the original building.

References: Gigs - 4th February, 6th July, 24th November 1983

Additional information: The February gig was the band's third ever gig and their first to be recorded and is widely available as a bootleg 'Live at The Hacienda'. The live version of "Handsome Devil" on the b-side of the debut 'Hand In Glove' single was taken from this concert. The band supported Factory funksters '52nd Street'.

The July gig saw the band perform neither with support or supporting another band for the only time in their history. Their final performance in November had the band travelling back from London after recording *Top Of The Pops* that afternoon promoting

the new single 'This Charming Man'. Support came from a very youthful 'James'.

At the rear of the building, there is a 'Hacienda Time Line'. Keep the railway viaduct on your right and walk to the end of the apartment building. Here, on your left, there is a narrow passageway leading to the Rochdale canal and the back of the building. At the end of the passageway, turn left and walk along until you reach 'The Hacienda Time Line'. There is a section of metal plates along the car park railings, each with a year and short details relating to that year in the life of The Hacienda. The 1983 plate simply says 'The Smiths', marking the three gigs played by the band that year.

THE RITZ, WHITWORTH STREET WEST

Directions: Facing The Hacienda apartments, turn

right along Whitworth Street West with the railway viaduct on your right. Continue on the left hand side of the road and after the traffic lights and bend in the road, The Ritz appears on your left. The Ritz is a ballroom with a 'spring set' dancefloor that moves up and down in unison with the heaving masses. The surrounding balcony upstairs gives it that truly ballroom feel, to a venue that opened in 1926 and was absolutely huge in the heady dance days of the late 20s and early 30s. It was also used as a brief location in the seminal 60s film 'A Taste Of Honey'.

The venue has hosted one of Manchester's best student /Indie discos since the early 1980s with it's Monday night 'Dance Yer Doc's Off', though is more cruelly synonymous with its 'Grab A Granny Night' reputation at weekends, attracting the slightly older women out on the town looking for a good night out!

Reference: Gig – 4th October 1982

Additional information: This was the venue of The Smiths very first concert, supporting 'Blue Rondo A La Turk.' The line up on the night was Morrissey, Johnny Marr, Mike Joyce and Dale Hibbert. Hibbert was a studio engineer and had helped the band with access to a recording studio and played on bass during sessions. It was his one and only gig as a 'Smith' before being replaced by Andy Rourke. Actually, there was a fifth member of the band that night too – James Maker. Maker was a friend of Morrissey and he was on stage acting as a dancer, playing maracas and a tambourine (pre-dating Bez from the Happy Mondays by a few years!) whilst reportedly wearing a smart suit and high heels, although Maker has always denied this. Maker went on to form the band 'Raymonde' whose song 'No One Can Hold A Candle To You' was covered by Morrissey in 2004 and indeed James Maker supported Morrissey on various dates during the same year with a band 'Noko 440'.

Morrissey also had another connection with The Ritz in that the band he fronted before The Smiths – The Nosebleeds (see Manchester Polytechnic) – played their second and final gig at The Ritz supporting Magazine in the summer of 1978.

THE PALACE THEATRE, OXFORD STREET

Directions: Facing The Ritz and turning right, you can see the theatre in front of you. A major venue for the big West End musicals ("Les Miserables", "Cats", "Miss Saigon", etc), with notoriously long and successful runs. The Palace made its grand opening on 18th May 1891.Though struggling to make a profit during the first few years, the management bowed to pressure and decided to book a less elitist repertoire and broadened its scope to include more popular performers, with resounding success.

During the early part of the 20th century it came

into its own with artists such as Danny Kaye, Gracie Fields, Judy Garland, Noel Coward and Laurel & Hardy stepping across its boards. During a nadir in his career, it is said that Frank Sinatra used to hang around in the foyer of The Ritz in an attempt to drum up custom for his one man shows at The Palace. In the 1970s, the theatre suffered the depression which bedevilled many, like its main rival the Opera House, failing to attract audiences in the wake of the spread of television.

The Palace was under constant threat of closure until the Arts Council stepped in to fund it in the 1980s, and after considerable internal refurbishment and an enlarged stage facility, it was - and still is - run by a charitable trust.

Reference: Gig – 31st March 1985

Additional information: The Smiths performed here promoting their 'Meat Is Murder' album, supported once again by James. The choice of venue was strange as, to my knowledge, no other band of such status has performed there previously or since. It was as if the band went out of their way to not to play traditional venues at the time such as The Apollo or The Gallery.

RAFTERS, OXFORD STREET

Directions: From the box office of the theatre, turn left walk up Oxford Street on the same side as the theatre. Immediately after the 'Stage Door' bar, you pass the vast St James Building. At the far end of the building, there are the twin venues of 'Jilly's' and 'The Music Box'. The St James Building housed a theatre within its walls from its opening in 1884. It became the first public venue in Manchester to show moving pictures in 1896 and it became a dedicated picture house in 1907 as The St James Picture House, although the location within the building of the cinema is not the same as the latter day nightclubs.

During the late seventies, Rafters became a key

venue on the punk scene. Its basement site was below Fagins – a discothèque which was a haven for hen parties and women dancing around in circles protecting their leather bags. Today, The Music Box occupies the basement whilst Jilly's is home to the upstairs rooms, regularly hosting all-nighters catering for rock, goth and indie genres on different floors.

Reference: Gig – 21st February 1983

The Smiths fourth gig, with the band booked to play between 'The Gay Animals' and the legendary New York punk Richard Hell And The Voidoids, who headlined.

Morrissey's time as a freelance gig reviewer for the weekly music press also ended at Rafters, when he reported for Record Mirror on a Depeche Mode concert in August 1980. The band were given the thumbs down, whilst local band Ludas – featuring Morrissey's friend Linder Sterling on vocals – were greatly praised!

SECTION 2
OXFORD ROAD & WILMSLOW ROAD

THE BBC MANCHESTER STUDIOS,
NEW BROADCASTING HOUSE, OXFORD ROAD

Directions: From The Music Box, head back down Oxford Street, past The Palace Theatre and crossing over Whitworth Street onto Oxford Road. Continue underneath the railway viaduct, over Charles Street and the studios are on your left.

This has been the home of the BBC in Manchester and the north west since 1976 - but not for much longer as the BBC are set to move into a new national media centre in Salford Quays which aims to open in 2011.

Reference: TV appearances - The Smiths - 10th February 1984 and 22nd February 1985

Additional information: The Smiths performed

on both nights in front of a studio audience on the BBC2's 'The Oxford Road Show', which was the BBC's answer to Channel 4's excellent 'The Tube' show, during a period when TV stations commendably and regularly featured live bands in programmes during peak viewing times.

The Smiths first appearance saw them performing 'What Difference Does It Make?' and the second appearance 'Shakespeare's Sister' and 'The Headmaster Ritual'.

MANCHESTER POLYTECHNIC STUDENTS UNION, 99 OXFORD ROAD

Directions: Continue down Oxford Street away from the city centre and on the same side as the BBC studios. In front of you is the 'Mancunian Way' flyover. Walk underneath the flyover and immediately on your left is the Manchester Metropolitan University Students Union building.

Back in the 70s and 80s, Manchester Metropolitan University was Manchester Polytechnic – or 'The Poly' as it was known. Regular gigs were held at the union building.

Reference: Gig –The Nosebleeds 15th April 1978

Additional information: Morrissey debuted as front man for The Nosebleeds at this venue, appearing at the bottom of the bill that included Salford's punk poet John Cooper Clarke and Wythenshawe's Slaughter & The Dogs.

This was a revamped line up of 'Ed Banger & The Nosebleeds' as Ed (Eddie Garrity) had left the band

and formed 'Ed Banger and His Group Therapy'.

Appearing alongside Morrissey in this new line up was guitarist Billy Duffy. Duffy was later credited with being the link between Morrissey and Marr coming together as he knew both individually. Duffy eventually joined Slaughter & The Dogs (whilst Morrissey unsuccessfully auditioned as their singer, with the microphone being given to Ed Banger rather ironically!) before eventually finding rock stardom in The Cult via 'Theatre Of Hate' and 'Death Cult'.

MANCHESTER UNIVERSITY STUDENTS UNION, WILMSLOW ROAD

Directions: Continue along Oxford Road, crossing over to the right hand side. Oxford Road becomes Wilmslow Road at the junction with Booth Street. Continue along Wilmslow Road, under the bridge with the university sign displayed on it. Eventually, the modern buildings are replaced by the older designs of Manchester Museum and Manchester University on your right, followed by the newer refectory and then the Union Building.

Not to be confused with the Metropolitan University Student Union – this building during term time is buzzing with students and is awash with fly posters and leaflets being handed out either promoting bands, club nights, student elections or student demonstrations.

The Academy 2 & 3 clubs are situated inside the building while the bigger Academy 1 is at the far end of the building just set back off the main road.

Reference: At the back end of the eighties the first ever Smiths conventions were held here, as hundreds of Morrissey-look-a-likes descended on Manchester from all over the world. The union building was host to various bands performing live, stalls selling memorabilia and coach tours of places such as The Iron Bridge, Salford Lads Club and Southern Cemetery etc. The world's very first 'Smiths Disco' was held in the evenings.

THE HOLY NAME CHURCH, WILMSLOW ROAD

Directions: Face the union building and turn around facing slightly to your right. Across the road is The Holy Name Church!

This large Catholic church was designed by Joseph Aloysius Hansom and although based on the 14th century French Gothic style, the foundation stone was laid in 1869. Opening on 15th October 1871, the imposing tower was added in 1928 – its darker colour stone clearly visible. During term time, the church appears somewhat lost surrounded by the rushed activities of the students, blending in as if part of the university itself. Yet out of term, the area is a ghost town!

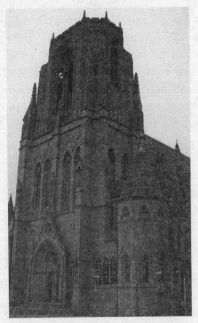

Reference: Lyrical – The opening line in The Smiths song 'Vicar In A Tutu' has Morrissey proclaiming:

'I was minding my business, lifting some lead off the roof of The Holy Name Church'

RUSHOLME / PLATT FIELDS PARK, WILMSLOW ROAD

Directions: Continue along Wilmslow Road towards Rusholme for a further 10 minutes or catch any of the many buses travelling in the same direction.

Passing the Manchester Royal Infirmary and Whitworth Park, you enter the district of Rusholme and the part of Wilmslow Road known as 'Curry Mile' due to the high density of restaurants and takeaways offering a great variety of Asian cuisine (definitely worth a visit during the evening). At the far end of Curry Mile, at the junction with Platt Lane, lies the vast Platt Fields, a municipal park complete with a boating lake.

Reference: The Smiths song 'Rusholme Ruffians' recounts 'The last night of the fair'. Fun fairs are held at various times throughout the year in the park. If you are lucky, the fair maybe there during your visit so you can see for yourself 'the grease on the hair of the speedway operator' or even take extreme action and 'jump from the top of the parachutes' - though, of course, I hope not, as you haven't completed the rest of the tour yet!

Return to the city centre via the regular buses on Wilmslow Road, alighting at Piccadilly Bus Station which is the last stop.

SECTION 3 - STRANGEWAYS...

ANN COATES

Directions: From Piccadilly Gardens, head up Oldham Street and continue away from the city centre to the top of the street where it meets Great Ancoats Street. The district of Ancoats lies behind the buildings across the road and to the right.

This district was the birthplace of the Industrial Revolution and many of the mills can still be seen today, though lying empty. However, the growing trend of city centre living has spread as far as Ancoats and many new developments are being undertaken, especially among the mills lining the Rochdale Canal.

Reference: What was a pun on the name of Ancoats, the elusive 'Ann Coats' was credited with backing vocals on The Smiths single 'Bigmouth Strikes Again' though, in truth, this was merely Morrissey's voice speeded up and dubbed onto the track!

PARKERS HOTEL, CORPORATION STREET

Directions: At the junction of Oldham Street and Great Ancoats Street, turn left onto Swan Street and continue straight past the CIS building (which is now Miller Street) and to the traffic lights at the junction of Corporation Street. The building across the road on your right with the green dome on top is Parkers Hotel.

The hotel was opened in 1915 but has recently been converted into individual apartments although the Parkers name remains.

Reference: The back cover of The Smiths 'Strangeways Here We Come' album. Go past the building on Corporation Street on the opposite side of the road and after 50 metres or so you reach the road sign (see picture). This is the exact position where photographer Stephen Wright stood when taking the picture that graced the back cover.

Myth Dispelling Time! As you will see, the sign in place today is different from the one taken back in 1987 and it has been consistently claimed (even in

this book's first edition!) that the original sign was taken as a souvenir by a fan shortly afterwards. The first time I came across the sign was in 1989 – two years after the album came out. Clearly there was damage to the sign as one corner had been snapped off but the original sign was still standing proudly.

The truth is all of the local signs were eventually replaced by more regional directing signs a few years later. Though of course, the image of a Smiths fan sat at home with the original sign hanging on his or her bedroom wall is far more romantic than the image of the council taking it down and throwing it on the tip, but who am I to tarnish the legend...

VICTORIA BRIDGE ROUNDABOUT, CHEETHAM HILL ROAD

Directions: Walk back to the traffic lights at the front of Parkers, cross over and turn right along Cheetham Hill Road, over the railway bridge towards the lights at the junction of Trinity Way / Cheetham Hill Road. This junction was formally a roundabout.

Reference: The opening scene on the promotional video for The Smiths single 'Stop Me If You Think That You've Heard This One Before' was taken at this junction, with Morrissey look-a-likes cycling across the top of the bridge and turning left down Trinity Way. As with the sign from the 'Strangeways' back cover, the local traffic directing sign has since been replaced by a more modern one.

The promotional video for 'Stop Me...' was changed

in the UK. The same film was used but to accompany the song 'I Started Something I Couldn't Finish'. Just prior to 'Stop Me...' being released in the UK, Michael Ryan went on the rampage in the Wiltshire town of Hungerford, killing sixteen people before adding his own name to the list of those who died that day. It was felt that the line in 'Stop Me....' that made reference to 'plan a mass murder' was too controversial and therefore the change in selection of the single was made, but using the same film to promote it.

STRANGEWAYS PRISON, SOUTHALL STREET

Directions: At the end of the bridge at the traffic lights, follow the road round to the right, continuing up Cheetham Hill Road on the left hand side. Take the third left, Carnarvon Street, following it down to the prison on Southall Street. At this point you are at the old prison gates.

The prison was opened in 1869 as Strangeways Gaol (Strangeways is the name of the district where the prison is situated) and the prison gained worldwide notoriety in 1990 after a forty day roof top demonstration following a riot. The prison was extensively rebuilt as a result of the riot and simultaneously renamed 'Manchester Prison' – though to Mancunians' and local media it will always be known as Strangeways!

References: The Smiths final studio album, released in 1987, was titled 'Strangeways Here We Come'.

The high walls of the prison were also used as a backdrop to the video 'Stop Me If You Think That You've Heard This One Before' with Morrissey briefly cycling around the prison walls, amongst other locations.

THE MANCHESTER EVENING NEWS ARENA, VICTORIA STATION

Directions: From the old prison gates, walk down Southall Street (with the wall on your right), past the new visitors centre to the end of the street, turning left onto Great Ducie Street, walking past the former Boddingtons brewery and turning left again at the traffic lights onto Trinity Way where the arena is in front of you. Cross over to the right hand side of the road and half way up Trinity Way there is a small set of traffic lights. At this point, on your right, there is a pedestrian subway underneath the arena clearly signed for the venue and box office.

The venue was officially opened (then called NYNEX Arena) on Saturday 15 July 1995 when

Torvill & Dean broke the UK box office attendance record for a single ice performance with over 15,000 fans in attendance. It became Europe's largest indoor arena and finally gave Manchester what it had desperately needed – an indoor arena big enough to host stadium bands that also had a decent sound system. The venue still has its critics (mainly from those sat right at the back or high up in the sides) but as much as we all love small intimate gigs, we sadly have to accept that the biggest bands and artists have to play in the biggest venues available.

Reference: Gig – Morrissey 22nd May 2004

Additional information: This was not only Morrissey's comeback gig after years in the wilderness without a record label or indeed a record to promote, but it was his first concert in Manchester since 1992, selling out in less than two hours. Performing on what was his 45th birthday, Morrissey was promoting the 'You Are The Quarry' album released in the UK the week before, Morrissey swept into town and swept all before him with a spectacular performance set to a 'Vegas' style lighted signage bearing his name.

The whole concert was eventually released in 2005 as the DVD, titled 'Who Put The M In Manchester?' The DVD single for 'First Of The Gang To Die' and the DVD for the live single 'There Is A Light That Never Goes Out' were also taken from this gig (although the CD recording for that single was recorded at Earls Court). Support came from Damien Dempsey and Franz Ferdinand.

Morrissey was also due to appear at the venue in 1995 when it was then known as 'The Nynex Arena'. He was due to perform on 6th December whilst touring with David Bowie but Morrissey had left the tour before it reached Manchester.

THE STAR & GARTER, FAIRFIELD STREET

Directions: From the MEN Arena, catch the Metrolink from Victoria Station across the city centre to Piccadilly Station (you may need to have to change at Piccadilly Gardens or Market Street). At Piccadilly Metrolink Station (which is below the main station), follow the signs leading to Fairfield Street and turn left out of the entrance walking along Fairfield Street, under the railway bridge to the traffic lights. Across the road you will see a pub - The Star & Garter - that plays host to the longest running Smiths and

Morrissey Disco in the world!

Built in 1877 and described in the *Manchester Evening News* as looking like 'Norman Bates house up the hill from the motel' (in the Hitchcock film 'Psycho') this pub downstairs/club upstairs venue is situated on the edge of a bleak, industrial estate that is also surrounded by a seedy red light district. Can there be a more appropriate venue to host a Smiths and Morrissey night? On the outside, The S'n'G itself looks derelict and ready for demolition, but on the inside the place is full of life during the monthly 'Smiths & Morrissey Discos'.

The discos are extremely popular with fans of all ages - from those who saw The Smiths live, reliving the glorious 80s to younger fans, including new students to the area. No matter what the age, everyone knows the words to each record played and everyone sings the words to each record played! Even after five hours of non-stop musical heaven, you still go home disappointed because one of your favourites wasn't played - or maybe it was but you arrived too late!

Close to the city centre, but far enough out and isolated from everywhere else, only those looking for a great night out venture down there. The nights are held on the first Friday of every month. For further information you can email Dave the DJ on <u>mozdisco@hotmail.com</u> and the club's website lists forthcoming dates of all their events at <u>www.starandgarter.co.uk</u> The nights start at 9.30pm and continue until 2.30am - a warm Mancunian welcome awaits you.

THE APOLLO THEATRE, STOCKPORT ROAD, ARDWICK GREEN

Directions: From the Star & Garter on Travis Street, you will see a curved shape building that Travis Street passes beneath. Follow the route under the building and immediately you will see a bus stop on your right as Travis Street meets London Road. From here, give your feet a rest and take the number 192 or 196 bus. This is a very short journey that will take you to the roundabout at Ardwick Green, where the Apollo Theatre stands at the junction of Stockport Road and Hyde Road. The bus stop is right outside the front entrance.

The well-trodden path to Ardwick Green has been taken for decades by local bands and fans alike. To play the Apollo was to have made it. The Apollo was built as a cinema, Manchester's biggest at the time, and opened in 1938, but was redeveloped in the late 70s to accommodate live bands.

Reference: Gigs - Morrissey, 15th December 1992 and 6th May 2006, 22nd & 23rd May 2009.

Additional information: The 1992 gig was Morrissey's one and only solo performance on home soil until the concert at the MEN Arena in 2004 - an absence of a staggering twelve years! Support came from The Well-Oiled Sisters.

Local fans did not have to wait anywhere as near long for future Manchester shows as the Apollo gig in 2006 was the first of three performances in the city over three consecutive days at three different venues! (see Opera House and Bridgewater Hall). Support came from Kristeen Young and Sons & Daughters.

Morrissey returned to The Apollo with two gigs over a weekend in 2009, the first being held on his 50th birthday, promoting his 'Years Of Refusal' album. Support came from 'Doll and the Kicks'.

Return to the city centre by catching the first bus heading that way from the opposite side of Stockport Road to The Apollo.

The Smiths also played one gig in Salford. Isolated from other places of interest listed, although not far from Manchester city centre, if you have the time this is how you get there.

MAXWELL HALL, SALFORD UNIVERSITY, THE CRESCENT, SALFORD

Directions: To get to the university, catch any of the buses 35-39 from Piccadilly Gardens. From the city centre, the buses soon join Chapel Street and then

The Crescent where shortly the university appears on your right hand side. The Maxwell Hall is inside the university itself so whether you will actually be able to get inside the hall depends if the university is open at the time of your visit.

Reference: Gig - The Smiths 20th July 1986

Additional information: This gig - the day after the G-MEX 'Festival Of The Tenth Summer' performance - was far more intimate and exclusively theirs. It also happens to be my all-time favourite gig by any band and fortunately it was recorded by students from the balcony and is today readily available to download via the internet. Support came from Factory band 'The Stockholm Monsters'.

On 4th November 2008, twenty-two years after the gig, Johnny Marr returned to the same venue for the first time and as a Visiting Professor, he gave a lecture to a packed Maxwell Hall on a the following topic:'Always from the Outside: Mavericks, Innovators and Building Your Own Ark'.

It was pleasing to hear Johnny - like myself - describe the gig here in July 1986 as his favourite Smiths gig.

To return to the city centre, catch the first bus back on the same side as the university.

THE GRAND TOUR

All that remains to be visited now are, in all honesty, the places you have spent years dreaming about visiting! This tour takes you a little further a field so there are two separate guides here, one for travelling using public transport and the other using a car. Information about each site is listed under the public transport section, so those in a car need to refer back at each site.

1. PUBLIC TRANSPORT

All but one of the sites are easily linked together by public transport on a circular route - the lone exception being The Salford Lads Club, the Mecca of all Smiths/Morrissey related places to visit.

SALFORD LADS CLUB, ST IGNATIUS WALK, ORDSALL

Directions: Take the No 33 bus from Piccadilly Gardens, a short journey through the city centre and onto Regent Road in Ordsall, you will reach the large Sainsbury's supermarket and retail park on your right. Going through the set of lights at the end of the supermarket, at the junction with Oldfield Road, immediately there is a bus stop - don't get off at this stop, get off at the next one! Walk in the direction that the bus was travelling for 50 metres and at the end of the fencing, West Crown Avenue appears. Turn left into the avenue and immediately in front of you is the Lads Club.

The famous entrance is at the very end of Coronation Street. Early scenes from the Granada TV soap opera 'Coronation Street' were filmed here in the early 1960s. The original Rovers Return pub was off the end of Coronation Street on Gloucester Street, named 'The Amalgamated Inn' it was demolished in 1971. Ordsall itself was the original Docks Estate where 'A Taste of Honey' was set and it is the 'Dirty Old Town' as written and sung about by Ewan MacColl (Kirsty MacColl's father) and latterly The Pogues.

The club was originally opened in August 1903 and officially opened in 1904 by Lord Baden-Powell and the building is in constant need of repair. In September 2001 the club applied for funding needed to keep the building open. The funding application was turned down, with the advice given that it would be cheaper to knock the building down and start again. Sacrilege!

It was made a listed building in August 2003 and is considered by English Heritage to be the finest example of a pre WWI Lads Club surviving in England. In 2005 it launched an appeal to raise £1m to restore and improve the building and to date (January 2007) it has raised in excess of £300,000 so it's beginning to look better for the long term future of the building.

The club still attracts more than 150 young people from Ordsall each week, with football, boxing and snooker being the main attractions. The club is now officially known as 'The Salford Lads & Girls Club' as girls have been admitted since 1994. The inside of the building has also been used frequently for TV and film backdrops. Former members include the actor Albert Finney, Eddie Colman, (a Manchester United footballer who tragically died in the Munich Air Disaster) the rock star Graham Nash, originally a member of Manchester's 60s band The Hollies but probably better known as one of the trio of Crosby, Stills and Nash. Also Allan Clark the lead singer of the Hollies and Peter Hook from Joy Division/New Order.

Reference: The Smiths once posed together outside the club in what became the now famous photo shoot, taken by Stephen Wright, that resulted in the glorious picture on the inside sleeve cover of 'The Queen Is Dead' album, released in 1986. The Smiths made another visit to the club and were pictured by Kevin Cummins when there was snow on the ground - in which Andy Rourke is seen sporting his streaked blond hair!

The original picture subsequently elevated the club into becoming the star attraction it is today. The entrance and surrounding area regularly gets a fresh coat of paint, wiping over the graffiti. Most of this graffiti, it has to be said, consists of lyrics from songs or other quotes from Morrissey or even Oscar Wilde!

The club and surrounding streets were also used as a backdrop for the promotional video to The Smiths single 'Stop Me If Think That You've Heard This One Before' in 1987.

The area has changed immensely since Morrissey and his look-a-likes cycled around the area during the video. At the time the vast majority of properties were boarded up, but have since been redeveloped. and while it looked like they were about to be demolished they were in fact being renovated. In 1987 the area became a tenants managed housing co-operative and is now one of the most successful co-operatives in the UK. So much so that Salford Council are about to designate the area a conservation zone. The club itself has changed its outward appearance as security gates has been placed in front of the entrance, (see picture).

On the weekend of Morrissey's MEN Arena comeback gig in May 2004, the club was besieged by fans from all over the world (indeed, your author ran two coaches full of fans travelling from Australia, USA, Canada, South America, Scandinavia and from all over Europe and the UK - even the NME came on board and gave the trip a whole page of coverage.) On the Friday night and Saturday afternoon The Smiths bass guitarist Andy Rourke teamed up with Vinny Peculiar and performed acoustic versions of two of Vinny's songs and three Smiths songs - 'Bigmouth Strikes Again', 'Ask' and 'Please Please Please Let Me Get What I Want'. Also on the Friday night, Linder Sterling set up her camera and filmed the night's events, some of which appeared on the 'Who Put The M In Manchester?' DVD, released the following year (including a short cameo appearance by yours truly outside the club!)

Also in 2004, the club opened up a room formerly used as a weight training room and converted it into a 'Smiths Room' full of pictures of fans stood outside the front of the building as well as news cuttings of the band relating to the building and artefacts or items of interest donated by band members or fans.

In January 2005 Vinny and Andy also played a live acoustic set broadcast on Salford Community Radio from the club band room. It was recorded for the Manchester District Music Archive:

www.mdmarchive.co.uk

In 2006, on the 20th anniversary release of 'The Queen Is Dead' album, The Smiths tribute band, 'The

Other Smiths' performed a set inside the main hall whilst Stephen Wright snapped pictures of fans outside the main entrance raising money for charity in the process.

The club has fully embraced the legacy left behind by that photo shoot and warmly welcomes visitors to the club - a far cry from 1986 when the club committee objected to the picture being used without permission and without royalties being paid. They lost the ensuing court case against the band and the then secretary of the club (a staunch royalist) was further incensed when he discovered the name of the album that the picture appeared on!

For those of you who love a bit of trivia - the club have an archive that includes over 15,000 membership records dating back to 1903. During a recent project they found the following

297 membership records with the surname Smith

27 membership records with the surname Morrissey

13 membership records with the surname Rourke

3 membership records with the surname Joyce

One membership record with the surname Marr (and 12 with the surname Maher).

The club has a website with information about exhibitions, open days and visiting the Smiths Room www.salfordladsclub.org.uk.

The full address for sending pictures or memorabilia is - The Salford Lads Club, St Ignatius Walk, Salford, Lancs, M5 3RX. After you have taken the obligatory picture outside the entrance, head back onto Regent Road, crossing over and taking the first bus back into Piccadilly, before catching the Metrolink, first to Old Trafford and then to Stretford, heading for Kings Road.

LANCASHIRE COUNTY CRICKET GROUND, TALBOT ROAD, OLD TRAFFORD

Directions: Catch the Metrolink on an Altrincham bound tram and alight six stops later at Old Trafford station. Go under the subway following signs for the cricket and football grounds. As you come out of the station, you are at the Old Trafford cricket ground. This site first hosted a game of cricket in 1857 as the Manchester Cricket Club, becoming the home of Lancashire County Cricket Club, playing their first game in 1865. Throughout the late 1990s the stadium has been redeveloped extensively in order to ensure lucrative international test matches and one day games are still played at the famous old ground. Indeed as I write, the club are about to embark on a large redevelopment programme.

Reference: Gig - Morrissey 11th July 2004

Additional information: Morrissey performed on the final night of the Move Festival. This popular 'Urban Glastonbury' ran for three consecutive years (2002-04), with Morrissey performing at a venue a mere stones throw from his old house on Kings Road. Five songs from this gig appear as extras on the 'Who Put The M In Manchester' DVD. Support came from James Maker (featuring Noko 440), The Ordinary Boys, The Beta Band and The New York Dolls.

MANCHESTER UNITED FOOTBALL CLUB, SIR MATT BUSBY WAY, OLD TRAFFORD

Directions: The football ground is also called Old Trafford and from the cricket ground, continue up Warwick Road at the side of the town hall, over Chester Road and onto Sir Matt Busby Way. The stadium opened in 1910 and has been extensively rebuilt over the past decade and is the biggest club stadium in England.

Reference: Morrissey's song 'The Munich Air Disaster 1958' refers to events in the club's history on 6th February 1958. The 'Busby Babes', as they were known, (Matt Busby was the manager of the young side) were returning from a European Cup game against Red Star Belgrade and stopped at the Munich-Riem airport for refuelling. After two aborted take offs, the plane crashed in a blizzard on its third attempt from an icy runway. Twenty-three of the forty three passengers on board the aircraft died in the disaster, including eight players and three club staff. The majority of the other casualties were journalists. The airport closed in 1992 and a plaque commemorating the disaster is displayed at the new Munich International airport.

As soon as you enter the forecourt of the football ground, look up towards your left and you will see the clock on the stadium wall and a plaque on the wall to the right of the clock - both commemorating the disaster and those who tragically died.

The song appeared as a B-side on CD2 of the single 'Irish Blood, English Heart' and a live version (following the 'Subway Train' intro) is on the 'Live At Earls Court' album.

384 KINGS ROAD, STRETFORD

Directions: Head back down Sir Matt Busby Way and Warwick Road towards the cricket ground, turning right along Talbot Road when you get there. Cross over onto the same side as the cricket ground and walk towards the first set of lights on Great Stone Road.

APPENDIX 1

You will see in front of you on your left, four identical office blocks. These are the offices of the Inland Revenue and Morrissey was employed here, in a clerical post, for a short period during 1977-78. At the end of one of Morrissey's many letters to the NME in the 1970s, he wrote 'PS I work for the Inland Revenue - am I still allowed to be a punk?'

APPENDIX 2

Opposite the furthest of the four Inland Revenue offices is North Trafford College. In the 70s this was Stretford Technical College and Morrissey attended here for one year, (1975-76) re-sitting his exams that he had not successfully passed at St Mary's School.

Turn left onto Great Stone Road.

APPENDIX 3

The B&Q store on your left was the site for a concert venue called 'The Hardrock' and in the 70s artists such as Marc Bolan and David Bowie performed here (Ian Curtis took his girlfriend and wife-to-be on their first date to see Bowie). In 1972, Morrissey had a ticket to see his beloved New York Dolls at the venue, but tragically during the band's first UK tour the original drummer, Billy Murcia, died after mixing alcohol and drugs and the remaining dates were cancelled - including the gig in Stretford. At The Move concert, Morrissey spoke of this 'non' event and stated that he still had the concert ticket in a shoe box!

Cross over to the right hand side of the road and at the roundabout bear right onto Kings Road. Morrissey's former house is on the right hand side just a few minutes walk away.

Reference: It was number 384 that Johnny Marr searched for in 1982 in the hope of finding a singer for a group he wanted to form. Minutes later Marr was in Morrissey's bedroom, the latter eventually handing over lyrics to some songs he had written, including Suffer Little Children. Marr had found his singer / song writer whilst Morrissey had found the musician for his lyrics. And the rest, as they say, is history!

THE IRON BRIDGE, KINGS ROAD, STRETFORD

Directions: Continue down Kings Road for a quarter of a mile on the same side as the house. Eventually you come to a row of four shops, with a gap in between the second and third shop (Nos 500 and 498). In this gap is the iron bridge!

Reference: The Smiths song 'Still Ill' contains the line

'Under the iron bridge we kissed,
and although I ended up with sore lips...'

Morrissey had come up with the lyric by rearranging a small section of lines from Viv Nicholson's autobiography, 'Spend Spend Spend' (Nicholson later appeared on the front cover of the single 'Heaven Knows I'm Miserable Now' and another picture was used on the UK promo only and

German release of the single 'Barbarism Begins At Home'. She also appeared on the band's 'South Bank Show' documentary.)

By pure coincidence, the bridge on Kings Road, crossing over the Manchester - Altrincham / Chester railway line (now the Metrolink line) is an iron bridge! Morrissey was a regular user of this bridge as at the far end to the right is a new housing estate, which was the site of St Mary's Secondary Modern School and his experiences there inspired the song 'The Headmaster Ritual'. Over the years, the bridge has 'acquired' a fair amount of Smiths & Morrissey graffiti as fans have left their messages for others to read.

If you do not wish to visit the cricket and football grounds, stay on the Metrolink at Old Trafford station and get off at the next stop, which is Stretford. Then proceed as follows:

After leaving Old Trafford station, keep your eyes alert, as the tram slows down to arrive at Stretford, as you pass under the iron bridge!

Come out of the station turning left onto Edge Lane. At the first set of traffic lights turn left again and you are now standing on Kings Road.

THE IRON BRIDGE

Directions: Walking along the left hand side of Kings Road, the house numbers start at 610, continue along until you reach a row of four shops. Between the second and third shop (Nos 500 - 498), is the iron bridge . See above for reference details.

SOUTHERN CEMETERY

Directions: From the foot of the bridge, continue up Kings Road in the same direction as before and on the same side of the road, closely following the house numbers until you reach the magical number of 384!

From either the iron bridge or 384 Kings Road, head in the direction as if you were walking from the house to the bridge (or catch a bus going in that direction) to the bottom of Kings Road and turn right towards Stretford Metrolink station and the bus stop is in front of you as the road rises. From here you can catch the following buses (heading for Stockport) direct to the cemetery situated on Barlow Moor Road: 23, 23A. The first entrance is for the crematorium, the second for the cemetery - the bus stop being just after the gates.

The cemetery opened on 9th October 1879 and has

increased in size for obvious reasons since then! The cemetery now continues on the other side of Nell Lane along Princess Road. There is also Manchester Crematorium, and Roman Catholic and Jewish cemeteries on the site.

Amongst the thousands of people buried in the cemetery are Sir Matt Busby (died 1994) (see Manchester United), L S Lowry (1976) - see Lowry Theatre, Tony Wilson, Factory Records supremo (2007), Marcel King (1995) singer of 70s Manchester group 'Sweet Sensation' and Billy Meredith (1958) legendary City & United footballer.

Reference: The Smiths song 'Cemetry Gates' (with Morrissey's infamous misspelling of the word 'Cemetery') opens with the line

'A dreaded sunny day,
so I'll meet you at the cemetry gates'.

It was at this cemetery that Morrissey and his close friend, Linder Sterling, paid regular visits, in which 'they gravely read the stones'. The song also quotes the names of the poets (Oscar) Wilde and (John) Keats as well as (William) Yeats. Linder had been a regular visitor to the cemetery long before she met Morrissey. When still named Linda Mulvey, she was sketching in the cemetery one day in July 1976, when she spotted a van parked outside advertising 'Malcolm McLaren presents The Sex Pistols'. A curious Linda ventured down to the Lesser Free Trade Hall (see Free Trade Hall) for the Sex Pistols second performance there (Morrissey attended both of them) - and from that night she unknowingly stepped into Mancunian Music Folklore, changing her name to Linder and being a leading light on the Manchester scene, designing sleeves for bands and fronting the band 'Ludas' (for more on Linder see 'Whalley Range').

How long you stay in the cemetery is entirely up to you. If you have the time and the weather is kind, then it is there for you to wander around. When you decide to leave, turn left at the entrance and walk in the same direction that the bus you came on was heading, turn left again at the major junction at Princess Road, a few hundred metres away. There is a bus stop as you turn the corner on your left. Catch any of these buses heading back into Piccadilly: 101, 104, 105, 109.

Here you have a choice. If you have the time, you can make a detour into Whalley Range and Hulme, if not simply remain on the bus all the way back to the city centre.

WHALLEY RANGE, 35 MAYFIELD ROAD

Directions: On the bus, ask the driver to drop you off at the beginning of Alexandra Park. You will be on the bus for a few minutes, passing the cemetery, Hough End playing fields and Whalley Range High School all on your left hand side. You will then pass another school sports playing field and reach some plush office buildings and it is here you need to alight, then walking in the same direction as the bus is going, towards the petrol station and the edge of the park. Here, on your left is a passageway, leading onto Demesne Road and you are now in Whalley Range. You now need to head off for Mayfield Road, so continue along Demesne Road until you reach the end of the park at the junction with Alexandra Road

South and turn right following the park. Cross over and Mayfield Road is the third road on your left. On Mayfield Road, keep on the left hand side, walking past St Bede's College (designed - like The Holy Name Church - by Joseph Aloysius Hansom in the 1870s), crossing over Alness Road until you reach number 35 at the far end of the road.

Once a middle class area of prosperity, today this district of wide roads with large Victorian houses has a very cosmopolitan population, combining the traditional white majority with black and Asian members of the community, students and a Bohemian crowd amongst its leafy lanes. In the late 70s the area had a reputation for being the heart of student bedsit land and the area to some extent was run down. However, with the recent property boom in south Manchester, the area has benefited from people not being able to afford to live in neighbouring Chorlton, but able to afford Whalley Range. This has attracted new developments to the area, though this in turn has the negative effect for locals in pushing the house prices up at the same time. The area also has the unwelcome reputation as being Manchester's main red light district.

Reference: The Smiths song 'Miserable Lie' contains the lines:

'What do we get for our trouble and pains?
Just a rented room in Whalley Range.
What do we get for our trouble and pains?
Whalley Range'

Morrissey was a regular visitor to 35 Mayfield

Road as this is the house converted into flats where Linder Sterling lived, sharing it with a few other musicians including fellow Ludas band members and John McGeogh - who played in Magazine, Siouxsie & The Banshees and John Lydon's Public Image Limited (John sadly died in March 2004).

Of course, Linder has remained very close to Morrissey since those bedsit days and in 1992 had a book published entitled 'Morrissey Shot' - producing exclusive pictures of Morrissey taken following him around on tour. As mentioned elsewhere, she also produced the documentary that accompanied the DVD 'Who Put The M In Manchester?'

HULME

Directions: Walk to the end of Mayfield Road and turn left on to Withington Road. Cross over and continue for around 200 metres until you reach the school where the bus stop is situated. Catch the 87 or 87a bus back into Piccadilly, via Hulme.

Hulme (pronounced hyoom) has had a number of face-lifts over the past few decades. Right on the edge of the city centre to the south, Hulme grew from farmland to become a densely populated district during the industrial revolution. The first Rolls Royce factory was in Hulme and the street names in the current Hulme commemorate this little piece of history - Royce Road and Rolls Crescent! By the start of the 1960s England had begun to remove many of the 19th century 'slums' and consequently, most of the slum areas of Hulme were demolished.

In Hulme, a new and (at the time) innovative

design for deck access and tower living was attempted, whereby curved rows of low-rise flats with deck access far above the streets was created, known as the 'Crescents' (which were, ironically, architecturally based on terraced housing in Bath).

High-density housing was balanced with large green spaces and trees below, and the pedestrian had priority on the ground over cars. At the time, the 'Crescents' won several design awards. However, what eventually turned out be recognised as poor design, workmanship, and maintenance meant that the crescents brought their own problems. Design flaws and unreliable 'system build' construction methods, as well as the 1970s oil crises meant that heating the poorly insulated homes became too expensive for low-income residents, and the crescents soon became notorious for being cold, damp and riddled with cockroaches and other vermin. As families moved out, squatters moved in, however, an increasing drugs, violent crime and prostitution problem in the area stretching into the 1980s made Hulme increasingly dangerous. Racial and social tensions in the area and neighbouring Moss Side culminated in race riots.

This final phase of decline prompted the 1990s regeneration of the area. A wholesale demolition and redesign of the area was implemented, including complete demolition of the 1960s "crescent" development, and replacement with conventional two-storey family houses with gardens, and small two and three storey blocks of managed apartments. Many of these properties were built by housing associations to provide the social housing necessary to rehouse many members of the local community, and a wide range of other different styles of property including apartments, townhouses and conversions of existing buildings were carried out by private developers for owner-occupation or renting by private landlords. The intention of this was to create a "mixed tenure" community, with owner-occupiers living side by side with council tenants, in order to create a more vibrant, diverse, and ultimately more economically successful neighbourhood. Changing the reputation of Hulme that was gained in the 1970's and 80's has been a long process, but one that appears to have been achieved.

Without being disrespectful to Hulme, there is nothing Morrissey related to get off the bus to actually see, so enjoy the ride back into town.

Reference: Morrissey lived in Hulme from his birth in 1958 until 1965, the family home being on Harper Street. The Morrisseys then moved to nearby Queens Square on the Hulme/Moss Side border, living there until 1969 when they took up residence on Kings Road in Stretford (see 384 Kings Road). The move to Stretford was taken as the council demolished entire sections of Hulme, as mentioned above, to make way for the concrete jungle that became known as 'The Crescents'. The Crescents make a brief appearance on the promotional video for The Smiths single 'Stop Me If You Think That You've Heard This One Before', where a Morrissey look-a-like is adjusting the back of his bicycle with the flats in the background. In 1990, Morrissey released a compilation of promotional videos for his early solo singles and he name checked the district, albeit with a witty pun, in the title of the compilation - Hulmerist.

APPENDIX 4

LOWRY THEATRE, PIER 8, SALFORD QUAYS

The Lowry Theatre is not only a venue for many forms of entertainment, it is also a tourist attraction in its own right. You could visit it on its own or as part of the Grand Tour, directions as follows.

Directions: For a return journey, from the city centre, catch the Metrolink on a tram heading for Eccles. You should alight at Harbour City, a few minutes walk from the venue. As part of the Grand Tour, after The Salford Lads Club, head back in to town and catch the tram to the venue as given above. To pick up the tour, journey back on the Metrolink - getting off at Cornbrook Station, catching the next Altrincham bound tram, getting off at Old Trafford station as the guide lists for Lancashire County Cricket Ground

Set in a magnificent waterside location at the heart of the redeveloped Salford Quays, The Lowry is an architectural flagship with a unique and dynamic identity. Rising from the regenerated docklands, it is a welcoming building, designed to reflect the surrounding landscapes and flourishing waterways, in its glass and metallic surfaces and is a fitting tribute to LS Lowry.

Laurence Stephen Lowry (1887-1976) was born in Manchester, although he is more associated with his pictures depicting Salford, where he lived and worked for well over thirty years.

Lowry is famous for painting scenes of life in the industrial districts of northern England during the early 20th century. He had a distinctive style of painting and is best known for urban landscapes peopled with many human figures 'matchstick men'. He tended to paint these in drab colours. Lowry declined an OBE in 1955, a CBE in 1961, a Knighthood in 1968, and The Order of the Companions of Honour in 1972 and 1976. He holds the record for the most honours declined!

The Lowry opened on 28th April 2000, bringing together a wide variety of performing and visual arts under one roof. The venue houses two main theatres and studio space for performing arts (1,730, 466 and 180 seats respectively) presenting a full range of drama, opera, ballet, dance, musicals, children's shows, popular music, jazz, folk and comedy and gallery spaces (1,610 metres of floor space) showing the works of LS Lowry alongside contemporary exhibitions.

A restaurant, cafes & bars are situated along the southern side of the building, with spectacular waterside views and in fine weather can extend out to quayside terraces overlooking the expansive Manchester Ship Canal.

Reference: Gig – Morrissey 18th April 2006

Additional information: Morrissey kicked off his thirty date UK tour promoting the 'Ringleader Of The Tormentors' album at the Lowry. Support came from 'Sons & Daughters'.

APPENDIX 5

PARK HOSPITAL, MOORSIDE ROAD, DAVYHULME

Directions: The hospital is a few miles away from any other sites on the tour but easily reached. Direct from the city centre, catch the No 256 from Piccadilly all the way to the hospital.

As part of The Grand Tour, by public transport, after the Iron Bridge/384 Kings Road, head down to the bottom of Kings Road, turning right onto Edge Lane, past Stretford Metrolink station and cross over to the opposite side of the road from the station. You then reach the busy A56/Chester Road, with the Stretford Arndale Centre on the other side of the road. Carry on straight over the A56 onto Kingsway (taking the subway is probably safer!) with the Arndale on your left and continue until you reach the bus stop and catch the No 256 bus to the hospital. To rejoin the tour, return the same way and make your way back to Stretford Metrolink station, then follow the directions for Southern Cemetery from the bus stop just past the station on Edge Lane.

Following the National Health Service Act of 1946, all municipal and voluntary hospitals were transferred to the state on July 5th 1948. On that day, the Right Honourable Aneurin Bevan, the Minister for Health, came to Park Hospital, Davyhulme to inaugurate the NHS by symbolically receiving its keys. On that day, Sylvia Beckingham was just 13 years old and the youngest person on Ward 5. It was by chance that Sylvia was chosen to be the first ever NHS patient when she met Bevan at the ceremony. An outbreak of measles on the children's ward meant that she had to be accommodated with adults in a glass sided veranda close to the hospital main entrance.

On the 5th July 1988, Sylvia Diggory (nee

Beckingham) returned to Park Hospital to unveil a plaque, commemorating its role in the foundation of the National Health Service and its re-naming as Trafford General Hospital. In July 1998 on the 50th anniversary of the NHS Frank Dobson - Secretary of State for Health, visited the hospital along with Sylvia Diggory to commemorate the anniversary.

Reference: Steven Patrick Morrissey was born here on 22nd May 1959.

End Of Tour

*

2. TRAVELLING BY CAR

SALFORD LADS CLUB
(POSTCODE FOR SAT NAV) M5 3RX

Directions: From the city centre, join the Mancunian Way heading westbound towards Salford/M602. Continue straight on as the Mancunian Way becomes Regent Road (A57 heading for Eccles). On your right there is a Sainsbury's supermarket - continue past it, through the traffic lights at Oldfield Road and then take the first left which is Gloucester Street. Immediately take the next right which is Coronation Street and the Lads Club is at the far end of the street on your left.

MANCHESTER UNITED FC - M16 0RA

Directions: Turn back down Coronation Street, Gloucester Street and onto Regent Road, turning left.

Continue in the left hand lane and at the roundabout turn left onto Trafford Road (A5063). Continue along and eventually you will see the stadium on your right. Go over the ship canal (the red bridge featured in the film 'A Taste Of Honey', where the two young lovers part for the final time as the bridge swings around) and follow the signs for Altrincham/Chester/A56 and onto Chester Road as you pass the White City Retail Park. Get into the right hand lane and turn right into Sir Matt Busby Way. As you reach the stadium, you can park on the right.

LANCASHIRE COUNTY CRICKET CLUB - M16 0PX

Directions: Turn back onto Sir Matt Busby Way in the same direction as you entered and go straight ahead at the lights over the A56 and onto Warwick Road at the side of the Trafford pub. At the lights further down, the cricket ground is in front of you.

384 KINGS ROAD, STRETFORD - M32 8GW

Directions: From Warwick Road, turn right onto Talbot Road (note the appendices included in the guide here) and left at the first set of lights onto Great Stone Road. Go over the railway bridge and onto the 'Quadrant' roundabout. Kings Road crosses the roundabout and take the third exit onto Kings Road and number 384 is a short distance down on your right hand side.

THE IRON BRIDGE
(0.2 MILES FROM 384 KINGS ROAD) - M32 8QW

Directions: Continue down Kings Road in the same direction as before, counting down the house numbers on your right until you reach No 498. Here you will find a small row of four shops and the bridge is in between the second and third shop.

SOUTHERN CEMETERY
(2.6 MILES FROM IRON BRIDGE) - M21 7GL

Directions: Continue again along Kings Road to the end and turn left onto Edge Lane (A5145) heading towards Chorlton. At the traffic lights, which is a forked junction, keep right remaining on Edge Lane. At the next set of lights turn right onto Barlow Moor Road (still the A5145) and after passing Chorlton Park on your left and a few shops, you reach the cemetery which is also on your left. The first entrance you reach is for the crematorium, the second entrance is for the cemetery itself. If the gates are closed, park in the side street opposite the gates.

WHALLEY RANGE
(2.7 MILES FROM SOUTHERN CEMETERY) - M16 8FU

Directions: Continue along Barlow Moor Road to the major junction with Princess Road (A5103) and turn left heading for the city centre. On your left you will pass the cemetery, Hough End playing fields and Whalley Range High School. Turn left as you reach the school at the lights at the junction of Wilbraham

Road. On Wilbraham Road, turn right at the first set of lights onto Alexandra Road South. Keep going, looking out for Alexandra Park on your right hand side with the junction of Demesne Road and from this point, still on Alexandra Road South, Mayfield Road is the third on your left. Go along Mayfield Road, crossing over Alness Road and No 35 is on your left hand side just before the end of the road.

HULME

Directions: At the end of Mayfield Road turn right onto Withington Road and continue straight ahead. Simply keep going and going straight on (Withington Road eventually becomes Chorlton Road) and this will take you through the redeveloped Hulme and onto the Deansgate roundabout at the end of the Mancunian Way and into the city centre where you began!

APPENDIX 6

THE LOWRY - M50 3AZ

Directions: If you wish to visit The Lowry, follow directions from The Salford Lads Club to Manchester United. Once on Trafford Road, turn right at the first set of traffic lights (the Lowry is well signed) and stay on that road within Salford Quays following the signs. You cannot park on the roads within the quays, but there is a multi-storey car park just before you reach the venue. To continue on the tour, head back to Trafford Road, turning right and picking up the directions for the football ground.

APPENDIX 7.

PARK HOSPITAL, DAVYHULME
(NOW KNOWN AS TRAFFORD GENERAL) - M41 5SL

Directions: From The Iron Bridge, go to the end of
Kings Road and turn right onto Edge Lane, going
over the humped bridge and down to the set of lights
at the A56/Chester Road junction with Stretford Mall
across the road. Go straight across the lights onto
Kingsway, heading for Urmston (B5213). Continue to
follow the signs to Urmston until you reach Urmston
Town Centre. From here, Trafford General Hospital
is clearly signposted. To return to the tour, simply
retrace the way you came, going back over the A56/
Chester Road at the Mall, past Stretford Metrolink
station and then continue past Kings Road where you
pick up the directions as given towards Southern
Cemetery.

The end of the tour as we know it.

THAT'S ENTERTAINMENT

OK, SO YOU have completed the tour, had your picture taken outside Salford Lads Club, ridden on the top of 'a double-decker bus' and 'gravely read the stones' in the cemetery.

Now what can you do?

Well, rather a lot actually! And this is where this guide can help you prepare for a great visit. By planning ahead, you can match your visit with a whole host of events to make it a truly memorable experience.

On arrival in Manchester, up-to-date information can be obtained from the *Manchester Evening News*, *Metro News*, or Manchester's Visitor Information Centre in the Town Hall Extension on Lloyd Street in the city centre.

MUSIC

The city boasts venues small, medium and large, catering for all musical tastes, whether a live concert or a club spinning top tunes into the early hours of the morning.

For live events, the mega-groups appear at

Europe's largest indoor arena at Victoria Station, currently named the Manchester Evening News Arena or the MEN Arena for short.

Tickets for most concerts tend to sell out quickly. Other major venues include the Apollo Theatre at Ardwick Green, the Academy, based at Manchester University and less frequently The Ritz on Whitworth Street West. Smaller venues are plentiful, namely the Roadhouse on Newton Street, Night & Day on Oldham Street or The Ruby Lounge on High Street. An honourable mention must also go to The Witchwood in Old Street, Ashton-under-Lyne, some eight miles east of Manchester city centre.

Piccadilly Box Office sells tickets for every venue in the area, indeed throughout the north west, with a small commission or booking fee payable on top of the ticket price.

You can access the Piccadilly Box Office online at www.ticketline.co.uk - 0161 832 1111. Tickets can be sent to you in advance or can be collected from the venue's box office. From this website, you can hyperlink into all of the venues in the area listed above to see who is performing in advance.

For those seeking their ideal club for a night of dancing, it would be impossible to list every club operating as clubs close, open and change hands frequently as well as changing styles to appeal to ever developing musical tastes. As mentioned, your best bet on arriving in the city is to pick up Friday's edition of the *Manchester Evening News*. Here, a complete review and preview of venues, style of music played and the all-important contact details are listed so you are sure to find something to suit your taste.

However, I can certainly recommend one club that you should try and plan your visit around and that is the monthly Smiths & Morrissey nights held at the Star & Garter www.starandgarter.co.uk on Fairfield Street and described more fully in the 'Around Manchester' section.

Five hours of pure heaven. What more could you ask for?

SPORT

Manchester is as famous for its sport as it is for its music, particularly football.

FOOTBALL (AUGUST - MAY)

Football is a religion in Manchester and Mancunians are fiercely divided in their support between their two football clubs. In fact, football was one of the few things that divided the close-knit Smiths! Both Morrissey and Andy Rourke are Reds (United), while Johnny Marr and Mike Joyce are Blues (City) - with Marr, as a promising youngster, even being offered schoolboy trials at City.

MANCHESTER UNITED

The name Manchester United is synonymous with Manchester throughout the world and attracts visitors from around the globe to the 'Theatre of Dreams'. The stadium at Old Trafford regularly hosts domestic and European games. It could be that your visit is planned around attending such a game. Understandably, given the huge demand, tickets are hard to come by and would have to be booked in advance. Despite being England's largest football club stadium, with a capacity of 75,000, each game is routinely sold out in advance. You could try your luck at the ticket office for last remaining tickets or the more riskier business of buying a ticket from 'unofficial sources' outside the stadium on match day – but you may be asked to pay more than the face value printed on the ticket.

However, the club also offers daily stadium tours, a 'Red Café', a museum, a hotel and a superstore open seven days a week. For further details, the club's website is www.manutd.com

To reach the stadium, take the Metrolink bound for Altrincham, alighting at Old Trafford. Please note the stadium right next to the station is also called Old Trafford, but hosts the game of cricket! The football stadium is a few hundred metres up the road.

MANCHESTER CITY

Since 2003, Manchester City have played home games in the new City Of Manchester Stadium (more commonly known as 'Eastlands'). The stadium was built for the 2002 Commonwealth Games, with a 34,000 capacity for the athletics events. This was then transformed into a 48,000 all-seated stadium for City to move from their famous Maine Road stadium, their home for 85 years. Maine Road, though much loved, had become outdated and the capacity reduced to 34,000. The opportunity to move into a new modern stadium for a fraction of the cost was too tempting to pass by.

You can reach the stadium by catching the 216 bus in Piccadilly to Droylsden/Ashton-u-Lyne. When the Metrolink expansion finally arrives, the trams will run right next to the stadium.

Tickets for most of City's games are easy to buy in advance and even on the day of the game itself.

Check the club's website www.mcfc.co.uk for more details.

There is a visitors centre and club store at the stadium.

*It must be noted that dates and kick-off times for both United's and City's fixtures frequently change, often at short notice, due to TV commitments, knock-out cup matches or on police advice.

Other teams playing league football in the Greater Manchester include Oldham Athletic, Bury FC, Stockport County, Wigan Athletic, Bolton Wanderers and Rochdale FC.

CRICKET (APRIL - SEPTEMBER)

That quintessential English game - the village green, a sandwich lunch and a pint of real ale! Well, you will not get any of that at Old Trafford Cricket Ground, but you will find a first-class game of county cricket watching Lancashire. Some one-day matches are 'Day-night' matches played under floodlights. Each year the venue also hosts international one-day and Test matches against the likes of Australia, South Africa, the West Indies, Pakistan, India, Sri Lanka and New Zealand. Tickets for these games do need to booked way in advance, but for domestic county matches you can turn up on the day. For further details visit: www.lccc.co.uk

To reach the stadium, take the Metrolink on the Altrincham line to the Old Trafford station, situated next to the cricket ground.

BASKETBALL (SEPTEMBER - APRIL)

Manchester Magic basketball team play their English National League games at The Amaechi Basketball Centre, Whalley Range High School For Girls, Wilbraham Road, Whalley Range.

www.magicbasketball.co.uk

Directions: Take the 101 or 109 bus from Piccadilly Gardens and alight at the junction of Princess Road and Wilbraham Road. The centre is inside the school which is on the opposite side of the road.

ICE HOCKEY (AUGUST - MARCH)

Manchester Phoenix play in the National League at the Altrincham Ice Dome. There should be no problem obtaining tickets on the day of a match.

www.manchesterphoenix.co.uk

To get there, take the Metrolink on the Altrincham line to the very last stop. The Ice Dome is right next to Altrincham station.

SPEEDWAY (APRIL - SEPTEMBER)

The Belle Vue Aces are one of the most famous speedway teams in the world. Racing at the Belle Vue Stadium, the Aces compete in the National Premier League and share the stadium with greyhound racing which also takes place weekly. Again, tickets are not required in advance, just turn up and enjoy the races!

www.belle-vue-speedway.co.uk

To get to Belle Vue, take the buses 201, 203 - 4 which stop right outside the stadium.

RUGBY UNION AND RUGBY LEAGUE

Both codes of rugby are popular in the Manchester area.

One of the country's leading Premiership teams, Sale Sharks Rugby Union FC moved out of their small compact Heywood Road home in Sale in 2003, and moved into Stockport County FC's Edgeley Park ground. Tickets shouldn't be too difficult to buy but best booking beforehand.

www.salesharks.com

Directions: Take a train from Piccadilly Station to Stockport station. Follow the signs to Edgeley Park from the station, which is a short walk away.

Meanwhile, you can catch the Salford City Reds Rugby League club playing in the Super League at the Willows Stadium, in the Weaste district of Salford. The club will be moving soon to a new stadium on the outskirts of Salford in Barton, next to the ship canal. Tickets can be bought on the day for the majority of games. For further details visit: www.reds.co.uk

To get to the Willows, take the No 66 bus direct from the city centre to the stadium.

SHOPPING

OF COURSE, SPORT isn't everyone's idea of entertainment. For many, simply walking through different shopping areas provides hours of pleasure in the search of an ideal bargain or souvenir of their visit!

Manchester, in common with every town and city throughout the country has been taken over by the multi-nationals. Walk down the main shopping streets and you could be in 'anywheresville'. They all have the same chains of American fast food outlets, music stores, electrical shops, travel agents, sportswear, clothes and shoes. There is no individuality left, very little consumer choice. The masses head for Market Street and the Arndale Centre while the posh folk seek out the exclusive labels around King Street, St Ann's Square and Deansgate.

So is there anywhere different to shop in Manchester? Of course there is! Manchester has a few golden nuggets for you to explore!

Afflecks Palace (though officially now called just 'Afflecks') is on the left-hand side of Oldham Street, while walking away from the city centre. Here you will find floors of independent traders selling everything alternative such as jewellery; clothes of all fashions including 80s, punk, goth, grunge etc; artists; tattooists; second-hand, vinyl and rare records, rock posters, postcards and t-shirts; vegetarian cafes; palm readers; aromatherapy oils and candles; stamp, old money and military memorabilia collectors and much more!

By the time you leave here, you could become the proud owner of a new Smiths t-shirt, as well as a Salford Lads Club poster, purchased that rare 12 inch single your collection was missing and bought a few Morrissey postcards to send to your jealous friends back home!

The success of Afflecks Palace has become a magnet for other small traders to operate around the former Affleck and Brown's Department Store. Piccadilly Records, a little further up on the left on Oldham Street, is the longest established independent record shop in Manchester.

Opposite Piccadilly Records is the excellent Café Pop, a retro bar decorated in sixties decor. Downstairs they also sell records, clothes and other items.

There are four second hand record/pop memorabilia shops in the city centre that are near to each other and well worth a visit.

Empire Exchange, 1 Newton Street

Vinyl Revival, 5 Hilton Street

Vinyl Exchange, 18 Oldham Street

Clampdown Records, 9 Paton Street

Shop until you drop, as they say, but remember to save your money for something to eat!

EATING OUT

Again, like Manchester's club life, restaurants come and go as quickly as a new guide is published. What you are guaranteed though is a restaurant catering for your choice of cuisine anywhere around the world! Again, Friday's *Manchester Evening News* publish lists of restaurants with contact details for easy reference. The city centre is full of eating establishments from the takeaway sandwich bars and traditional English fish and chip shops, to pubs serving food and restaurants both cheap and not so cheap!

Restaurants and pubs are scattered around the city centre, but there are four areas that excell in providing choice, quality and an experience to remember!

Chinatown, in the heart of the city centre needs no explanation. The area centred around the Chinese Arch on the Faulkner Street and Nicholas Street junction has literally dozens of establishments for you to choose from.

Across Portland Street from Chinatown is the vibrant Gay Village (see Manchester Today section). Here a great selection of restaurants, especially on Canal Street, have opened up. Built around a thriving scene, the area is one of Manchester's modern day success stories of turning urban decay into a multi-million pound success story.

The third district, is a few miles outside of the city centre and is the wonderful Rusholme (see Around Manchester tour).

Rusholme brings you the best from the Indian sub-continent and is only bettered in England by Bradford, in West Yorkshire. The ever thriving Wilmslow Road, a busy corridor for city centre commuters and students alike during the day, is transformed into 'Curry Mile' in the evening with the smell of the spices overpowering the fumes from the passing vehicles! Some restaurants are licensed to serve alcohol on the premises; some do not have a license, but allow you to take your own alcohol in to consume with your meal.

A few, for religious reasons, do not allow alcohol to be consumed on the premises, so please check before entering so as not to cause offence. There are takeaway bars as well as restaurants along Wilmslow Road.

To get to Rusholme, jump on any of the buses numbered 40 - 49 from Piccadilly and trust me, you will know when you are there!

Finally, the ever improving Northern Quarter has seen many bars and eateries open over the past few years. The area lies between Afflecks and Shudehill and all the side streets surrounding them (Thomas Street being the main hub.)

VEGETARIAN FOOD

Most, if not all restaurants throughout the city, cater for vegetarians, however, there are a few vegetarian and vegan establishments well worth a try!

One, the Eighth Day Café, has been established on Oxford Road opposite the Metropolitan University since the early 1970's. Here, as well as a café, they also have a shop serving snacks and food to take with you as well as a range of animal-free goods such as health products and toiletries along with related magazines and gifts. You actually pass the Eighth Day Café on the 'Around Manchester' tour - it is situated next to the Metropolitan University Student Union building and a warm welcome always awaits you!

One thing you can be guaranteed is wherever you do chose to eat, your taste buds are in for a treat!

COMEDY

Manchester has always been up for a laugh, as the birthplace of comedians such as Les Dawson, Bernard Manning, Caroline Aherne, Craig Cash and Steve Coogan. So, if you fancy a laugh, the following clubs should provide plenty:

THE COMEDY STORE

London's famous club has travelled north and resides at Deansgate Locks, underneath the elevated G-Mex Metrolink station.

www.thecomedystore.co.uk

THE FROG AND BUCKET.

Situated at the top end of Oldham Street and Great Ancoats Street.

CINEMA

There are a three cinemas in the city centre. The Filmworks at the Printworks complex on Shudehill boasts 20 screens and a huge IMAX screen.

The Great Northern development on the corner of Peter Street and Deansgate houses the AMC Cinema with its 16 screens.

The Cornerhouse on the bottom of the approach road to Oxford Road Station screens classic films and non-mainstream or 'arthouse' films.

THEATRE

After London's West End, Manchester is the place to be, in thespian circles that is! All the big touring shows perform in the city, either at the Palace Theatre on Oxford Street or the Opera House on Quay Street. For further details on both venues visit
www.manchestertheatres.co.uk

Smaller venues hosting more locally produced shows include:

The Library Theatre, based in Manchester's Central Library in St Peters Square
www.libtheatreco.org.uk

The Royal Exchange Theatre on St Ann's Square
www.royalexchange.co.uk

The Lowry in Salford Quays: www.thelowry.com

The Contact Theatre at Manchester University.
www.contact-theatre.org.uk

MUSEUMS AND ART GALLERIES

Again, you are spoilt for choice, with the Science and Industry Museum on Liverpool Road, Castlefield, charting the Industrial Revolution and the Manchester Museum based at the University on Wilmslow Road.

There are also several art galleries: The City Art Gallery on Mosley Street, the Whitworth Art Gallery on the edge of Rusholme on Wilmslow Road, the Lowry Centre at Salford Quays and The Cornerhouse opposite the Palace Theatre.

There is the Pump House: People's History

Museum on Bridge Street, and the Pankhurst Centre in Nelson Street, Victoria Park, dedicated to the Women's Suffrage movement.

There is also a Chinese Arts Centre, Irish Heritage Centre in and a Manchester Jewish Museum too.

CLASSICAL MUSIC

Visit the home of The Halle Orchestra, The Bridgewater Hall on Lower Mosley Street.
<u>www.bridgewater-hall.co.uk</u>

BIBLIOGRAPHY

I SWEAR I WAS THERE
David Nolan (MILO Books)

MANCHESTER ENGLAND
Dave Haslam (Fourth Estate)

MORRISSEY AND MARR:
THE SEVERED ALLIANCE
Johnny Rogan (Omnibus Press)

SHAKE RATTLE AND RAIN
C P Lee (Hardinge Simpole)

THE SMITHS: SONGS
THAT SAVED YOUR LIFE
Simon Goddard (Reynolds & Hearn)

LOCATIONS INDEX

THE MANCHESTER MUSICAL HISTORY TOUR

BY PHILL GATENBY & CRAIG GILL

THE MANCHESTER MUSICAL HISTORY TOUR

PHILL GATENBY & CRAIG GILL

ISBN: 1901746 712 - 9781901746716

£7.95 - PAPERBACK - 160pp

PUBLISHED: 1st NOVEMBER 2010

SPECIAL OFFER - GET THE BOOK FOR JUST £6 - POST FREE
Call 0161 872 3319 or www.empire-uk.com

From the late 1950's, Mancunians have had a passion for creating and following great music. Be it live or via recordings, the city centre has been a magnet for generations of locals – and in recent years music fans from all over the country and beyond – to enjoy.

Whilst cities such as Liverpool and Memphis turned their musical heritage into a tourist attractions, Manchester kept looking forward, developing new scenes and tastes. Yet the 2002 film 'Twenty-Four Hour Party People' was probably the point at which Manchester music fans started to look back at the rich musical history of their city. This coincided with the publication of the book 'Morrissey's Manchester" by Phill Gatenby, also in 2002 and numerous other publications penned by luminaries of the Manchester scene.

Following the success of Morrissey's Manchester, a guide book dedicated to locations associated with The Smiths, author Phill Gatenby has put together several tours featuring other world famous Manchester bands from the Buzzcocks via Joy Division to Oasis, Elbow and Doves as well as the various scenes from beat to acid house or even lo-fi.

An interesting guide for anyone with an interest in British music, the guide documents the various clubs and venues that have influenced Manchester based musicians over the last 50 years.

GRAFTING FOR ENGLAND
THE INSIDE STORY OF ENGLAND ABROAD
IN HOOLIGANISM'S GOLDEN AGE

ISBN: 1901746 658 - 9781901746655

£8.95 - Softback - 224 pp

Published: June 2010

The early 1980s was a golden age for football hooliganism and shoplifting in Europe. With security forces on the continent yet to fully realise the extent of the English Disease and security relaxed in even the most expensive shops. The continent was ripe for pillage and Sully was one of many to take full advantage - funding his trips following the national team with ill-gotten gains.

As a member of Manchester City's notorious Mayne Line Service Crew he was accustomed to far stricter security in England. Using the cover of fellow England fans Tony reveals the secrets of his success in ' Grafting for England' the follow-up to 'Sully - the football thug who didn't give a fuck' published by Empire last year.

As Tony makes clear, the football wars in England didn't necessarily stop when hooligans from all over the country got together to follow the national side. Fights would regularly be sparked off between different factions supporting the Three Lions and even a trip to Wembley could catch unsuspecting patriots unawares.

Sully has followed England over most of the continent for the best part of 30 years - from the notorious 1980 European Championship where the England team were forced to play through a cloud of tear gas, to the slaughter of the innocents in Rome in the late 90s, where Italian scooter boys slashed anyone looking remotely English. The hairiest moments though are reserved for trips into the former Soviet Bloc with the Poles, in particular, lending a unique lunacy to trips to Chorzow and Warsaw.

In between Sully recalls his frequent inactive periods at Her Majesty's Pleasure including his involvement in the notorious Strangeways Riot and the demise of his grafting career abroad following the confiscation of his passport. Of course, it being Sully, comedy is never far away particularly when lads' trips to Greece and Portugal don't go quite as planned.

BOOKS BY THE SAME AUTHOR

SULLY

THE INSIDE STORY OF MANCHESTER CITY'S

NOTORIOUS MAYNE LINE SERVICE CREW

ISBN: 1901746534

£8.95 - Softback - 224 pp

SPECIAL OFFER - GET THE BOOK FOR JUST £6 - POST FREE
Call 0161 872 3319 or www.empire-uk.com

FOR ALMOST 25 YEARS, Tony Sullivan has been a member of some of the most violent gangs following Manchester City. He has also toured Britain and Europe as a professional 'grafter'. Sullivan ran with the Mayne Line Motorway Service Crew in the early 80s. Here he details how they gained a fearsome reputation nationwide. From St James' Park to Upton Park, the Mayne Line ruled British football, the most fearsome football mob during, hooliganism's 'Golden Age'.

Now, with his hooligan career at a close, 'Sully' looks back on this violent era and relives the good hidings handed out and the kickings received. He also details some of the stunts he and his mates pulled - using the cover of his fellow fans to 'earn' a living in an era before extensive CCTV surveillance, often with unexpected results.

Along the way he contrasts the exploits of the various supporters groups he encountered - the scouser's well known propensity for using a blade, the United supporter's unwillingness to take part in a fight unless they were certain to win it and the craziness of a typical away day in Newcastle city centre in the early eighties.

Later, as police cracked down on hoolganism, many left the scene and the Mayne Line disbanded. Still Sully carried on regardless, the violence and buzz still a 'drug'. Unfortunately, several custodial sentences curtailed his career including, in 1991, an incidental involvement in the Strangeways Riot and its aftermath.

The 1990s also saw a slew of hooligan memoirs hit the nation's bookshelves, often written by people with tenuous connections to the incidents described. Others sought to celebrate hooligan culture as somekind of weekly fashion parade. Sully has little time for either as he explains:

"Over the years I have been beaten, stabbed, had bottles cracked on my head and had lads threatening to come round my gaff - but you wont hear me complain.This book is a true account of those years, devoid of sensational bullshit."
'SULLY'

Reminiscences Of Manchester
And Its Surrounding Areas From 1840
by Louis M Hayes

£12.95 - Paperback - 384pp

ORIGINALLY PUBLISHED 1905
TO BE RE-PUBLISHED: JULY 2009

SPECIAL OFFER - GET THE BOOK FOR JUST £9 - POST FREE
Call 0161 872 3319 or www.empire-uk.com

Written over the course of his lifetime, Louis Hayes' memoirs of Manchester life 'Reminiscenes of Manchester' is an evocative memoir of the city's formative years. Beginning in 1840, Hayes recalls a Manchester where the countryside began at Strangeways and farms dotted the surrounding areas.

During the course of his lifetime he saw Manchester grow from industrial new town to international trading centre. The story of this growth and recognition comes across in his writings, originally intended as a memoir for his family, that acts as a valuable historical document. Besides outlining the social changes in the city, Hayes profiles the key characters, prominent MPs, social reformers and members of the legal profession, many he knew personally, who made a mark in Manchester life between the years 1840 and 1905.

Hayes also chronicles the various triumphs and crises that hit Manchester in this period - the Great Flood of 1866, Queen Victoria's State Visit of 1853 that conferred city status on Manchester, the Great Treasures Exhibition of 1857 and the Cotton Famine of the 1860s brought on by the American Civil War. The author also outlines the impact made by immigrants to the city, the various traders from the Far and Near East that made an impact on Mancunian trade and society. He also documents the characters prevalent in the theatre during this period, and the 'fads' of Manchester society from popular music to amusements.

An invaluable guide to those keen to know more about the formative years of the city and those who wonder what life was like for Mancunians over a century ago, Reminiscences of Manchester is a remarkable work re-printed here in full with additional footnotes and the illustrations published in the First Edition.

THE CARPET KING OF TEXAS
PAUL KENNEDY

ISBN: 1901746 666 - 9781901746662
£8.95 - PAPERBACK - 295 PP
PUBLISHED: 1ST OCTOBER 2010

**"TRAINSPOTTING FOR THE
VIAGRA GENERATION"**
SUNDAY MIRROR
**"DRUG-TAKING, SEXUAL DEPRAVITY...
NOT FOR THE FAINT HEARTED."**
NEWS OF THE WORLD

This shocking debut novel from award-winning journalist Paul Kennedy tells the twisted tales of three lives a million miles apart as they come crashing together with disastrous consequences.

Away on business, Dirk McVee is the self proclaimed "Carpet King of Texas" - but work is the last thing on his mind as he prowls Liverpool's underbelly to quench his thirst for sexual kicks.

Teenager Jade Thompson is far too trusting for her own good. In search of a guiding light and influential figure, she slips away from her loving family and into a life where no one emerges unscathed.

And John Jones Junior is the small boy with the grown-up face. With a drug addicted father, no motherly love, no hope, and no future, he has no chance at all.

The Carpet King of Texas is a gritty and gruesome, humorous and harrowing story of a world we all live in but rarely see.

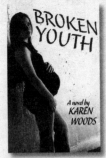

BROKEN YOUTH
A novel by Karen Woods

ISBN: 1901746 631 - 9781901746631

£8.95 - PAPERBACK - 224 PP

PUBLISHED: 1ST MARCH 2010

"Sex , violence and fractured relationships, a kitchen sink drama that needs to be told and a fresh voice to tell it." TERRY CHRISTIAN

When rebellious teenager Misty Sullivan falls pregnant to a local wannabe gangster, she soon becomes a prisoner in her own home. Despite the betrayal of her best friend, she eventually recovers her self-belief and plots revenge on her abusive boyfriend with spectacular consequences.

This gripping tale sees the impressive debut of Karen Woods in the first of a series of novels based on characters living on a Manchester council estate. Themes of social deprivation, self-empowerment, lust, greed and envy come to the fore in this authentic tale of modern life.

SPECIAL OFFER - GET THESE BOOKS FOR JUST £7 - POST FREE
Call 0161 872 3319 or www.empire-uk.com

BLACK TEARS
A NOVEL BY KAREN WOODS

ISBN: 1901746 720 - 9781901746723

£8.95 - PAPERBACK - 224 PP

PUBLISHED: 1ST NOVEMBER 2010

"MANCHESTER'S ANSWER TO MARTINA COLE"

With evil Gordon locked up in Strangeways for 5 years, the characters from Karen Woods' debut novel 'Broken Youth' come to terms with life without him.

Misty, now married to Dominic, gives birth to Gordon's child, Charlotte. Her former best friend Francesca also gives birth to one of Gordon's children, Rico, while staying with Gordon's heroin addicted brother Tom.

Meanwhile, as the clock ticks down on his sentence, Gordon broods on the injustice of his situation and plots sweet revenge on those on the outside.

COMPLETIST'S DELIGHT - THE FULL EMPIRE BACK LIST

ISBN	TITLE	AUTHOR	PRICE	STATUS¹
1901746003	SF Barnes: His Life and Times	A Searle	£14.95	IP
1901746011	Chasing Glory	R Grillo	£7.95	IP
190174602X	Three Curries and a Shish Kebab	R Bott	£7.99	IP
1901746038	Seasons to Remember	D Kirkley`	£6.95	IP
1901746046	Cups For Cock-Ups+	A Shaw	£8.99	OOP
1901746054	Glory Denied	R Grillo	£8.95	IP
1901746062	Standing the Test of Time	B Alley	£16.95	IP
1901746070	The Encyclopaedia of Scottish Cricket	D Potter	£9.99	IP
1901746089	The Silent Cry	J MacPhee	£7.99	OOP
1901746097	The Amazing Sports Quiz Book	F Brockett	£6.99	IP
1901746100	I'm Not God, I'm Just a Referee	R Entwistle	£7.99	OOP
1901746119	The League Cricket Annual Review 2000	ed. S. Fish	£6.99	IP
1901746143	Roger Byrne - Captain of the Busby Babes	I McCartney	£16.95	OOP
1901746151	The IT Manager's Handbook	D Miller	£24.99	IP
190174616X	Blue Tomorrow	M Meehan	£9.99	IP
1901746178	Atkinson for England	G James	£5.99	IP
1901746186	Think Cricket	C Bazalgette	£6.00	IP
1901746194	The League Cricket Annual Review 2001	ed. S. Fish	£7.99	IP
1901746208	Jock McAvoy - Fighting Legend *	B Hughes	£9.95	IP
1901746216	The Tommy Taylor Story*	B Hughes	£8.99	OOP
1901746224	Willie Pep*+	B Hughes	£9.95	OOP
1901746232	For King & Country*+	B Hughes	£8.95	OOP
1901746240	Three In A Row	P Windridge	£7.99	IP
1901746259	Viollet - Life of a legendary goalscorer+PB	R Cavanagh	£16.95	OOP
1901746267	Starmaker	B Hughes	£16.95	IP
1901746283	Morrissey's Manchester	P Gatenby	£5.99	IP
1901746313	Sir Alex, United & Me	A Pacino	£8.99	IP
1901746321	Bobby Murdoch, Different Class	D Potter	£10.99	OOP
190174633X	Goodison Maestros	D Hayes	£5.99	OOP
1901746348	Anfield Maestros	D Hayes	£5.99	OOP
1901746364	Out of the Void	B Yates	£9.99	IP
1901746356	The King - Denis Law, hero of the...	B Hughes	£17.95	OOP
1901746372	The Two Faces of Lee Harvey Oswald	G B Fleming	£8.99	IP
1901746380	My Blue Heaven	D Friend	£10.99	IP
1901746399	Viollet - life of a legendary goalscorer	B Hughes	£11.99	IP
1901746402	Quiz Setting Made Easy	J Dawson	£7.99	IP
1901746410	The Insider's Guide to Manchester United	J Doherty	£20	IP
1901746437	Catch a Falling Star	N Young	£17.95	IP
1901746453	Birth of the Babes	T Whelan	£12.95	OOP
190174647X	Back from the Brink	J Blundell	£10.95	IP
1901746488	The Real Jason Robinson	D Swanton	£17.95	IP
1901746496	This Simple Game	K Barnes	£14.95	IP
1901746518	The Complete George Best	D Phillips	£10.95	IP
1901746526	From Goalline to Touch line	J Crompton	£16.95	IP
1901746534	Sully	A Sullivan	£8.95	IP

1901746542	Memories...	P Hince	£10.95	IP
1901746550	Reminiscences of Manchester	L Hayes	£12.95	IP
1901746569	Morrissey's Manchester - 2nd Ed.	P Gatenby	£8.95	IP
1901746577	The Story of the Green & Gold	C Boujaoude	£10.95	IP
1901746585	The Complete Eric Cantona	D Phillips	£10.95	IP
1901746593	18 Times	J Blundell	£9.95	IP
1901746 607	Old Trafford - 100 Years	I McCartney	£12.95	IP
1901746615	Remember Me	K C Kanjilal	£7.95	IP
1901746623	The Villa Premier Years	S Brookes	£8.95	IP
1901746631	Broken Youth	K Woods	£8.95	IP
190174664X	The Devil's Dust	B Yates	£9.95	IP
1901746658	Grafting for England	T Sullivan	£8.95	I{
1901746666	The Carpet King of Texas	P Kennedy	£8.95	IP
1901746704	Manchester United Premier Years	S Brookes	£8.95	IP

* Originally published by Collyhurst & Moston Lads Club + Out of print PB Superceded by Ppb edition

† In Print/Out Of Print/To Be Published (date)